WITTGENSTEIN AND THE MYSTICAL

Philosophy as an Ascetic Practice

American Academy of Religion
Reflection and Theory in the Study of Religion

Editor
David E. Klemm

Number 02
WITTGENSTEIN AND THE MYSTICAL
Philosophy as an Ascetic Practice
by
Frederick Sontag

WITTGENSTEIN AND THE MYSTICAL

Philosophy as an Ascetic Practice

by
Frederick Sontag

Scholars Press
Atlanta, Georgia

WITTGENSTEIN AND THE MYSTICAL
Philosophy as an Ascetic Practice

by
Frederick Sontag

© 1995
The American Academy of Religion

Library of Congress Cataloging in Publication Data
　Wittgenstein and the mystical : philosophy as an ascetic practice
/ by Frederick Sontag.
　　　p.　cm. — (AAR reflection and theory in the study of religion ; no. 02)
　Includes bibliographical references and index.
　　　ISBN: 978-1-55540-993-7

　1. Wittgenstein, Ludwig, 1889–1951. I. Title. II. Series.
B3376.W564S625　1995
192—dc20　　　　　　　　　　　　　　94-30657
　　　　　　　　　　　　　　　　　　CIP

Printed in the United States of America
on acid-free paper

For
C. S. K.

*You will learn the truth
and the truth will make
you free.*

John 8: 32
The Jerusalem Bible

Other Books by Frederick Sontag

Divine Perfection: Possible Ideas of God, 1962

The Existentialist Prolegomena: To a Future Metaphysics, 1969

The Future of Theology: A Philosophical Basis for Contemporary Protestant Theology, 1969

The Crisis of Faith: A Protestant Witness in Rome, 1969

The God of Evil: An Argument from the Existence of the Devil, 1970

God, Why Did You Do That?, 1970

The Problems of Metaphysics, 1970

How Philosophy Shapes Theology: Problems in the Philosophy of Religion, 1971

The American Religious Experience: The Roots, Trends and the Future of American Theology (with John K. Roth), 1972

Love Beyond Pain: Mysticism Within Christianity, 1977

Sun Myung Moon and the Unification Church, 1977

God and America's Future (with John K. Roth), 1977

What Can God Do?, 1979

A Kierkegaard Handbook, 1979

The Elements of Philosophy, 1984

The Questions of Philosophy (with John K. Roth), 1988

Emotion: Its Role in Understanding and Decision, 1989

The Return of the Gods: A Philosophical/Theological Reappraisal of the Works of Ernest Becker, 1989

Uncertain Truth, 1995

Forthcoming

The Descent of Woman

The Acts of the Trinity

Not everything can be named.
Some things draw us beyond words.

Aleksandr I. Solzhenitsyn
in *Nobel Lecture on Literature*

There is indeed the inexpressible,
this *shows* itself;
it is the mystical.

Ludwig Wittgenstein
Tractatus 6.522

Table of Contents

Preface xi

Chapter 1

Philosophical Themes in Wittgenstein's Life 1
   A. Ten Themes 1
   B. Biography and Philosophy 4
   C. "Vain are the words of the philosopher...
      if they heal no suffering of man." 6

Chapter 2

From the Rigor and Clarity of Logic to the Ineffability and
Struggle of the Spirit 9
   A. The *Tractatus* as a Philosophy of Finality 9
   B. The *Investigations*
      as the De-systematization of Philosophy 11
   C. Philosophy as Detached Utterance:
      The Blue & the Brown Books 14
   D. Certainty and Religion 16
   E. Philosophy in a Wider Context 19
   F. Sophisticated Trivializing 27
   G. The Importance of the Momentary and the Random .. 33
   H. Color, and Psychology, and States of Mind 40

Chapter 3

Wittgenstein and Some of His Interpreters 45
   A. Finality and Non-Finality in Philosophy 45
   B. Completing Wittgenstein 49
   C. Ayer and Positivism 50
   D. "Wittgenstein's Conception of Philosophy" 52

Chapter 4

Wittgenstein and His Biographers 59
   A. How Biography Illuminates Language 59
   B. Monk: Life at the Border 69

TABLE OF CONTENTS

Preface xi

CHAPTER 1

Philosophical Themes in Wittgenstein's Life 1
   A. Ten Themes 1
   B. Biography and Philosophy 4
   C. "Vain are the words of the philosopher...
       if they heal no suffering of man." 6

CHAPTER 2

From the Rigor and Clarity of Logic to the Ineffability and
Struggle of the Spirit 9
   A. The *Tractatus* as a Philosophy of Finality 9
   B. The *Investigations*
       as the De-systematization of Philosophy 11
   C. Philosophy as Detached Utterance:
       The Blue & the Brown Books 14
   D. Certainty and Religion 16
   E. Philosophy in a Wider Context 19
   F. Sophisticated Trivializing 27
   G. The Importance of the Momentary and the Random .. 33
   H. Color, and Psychology, and States of Mind 40

CHAPTER 3

Wittgenstein and Some of His Interpreters 45
   A. Finality and Non-Finality in Philosophy 45
   B. Completing Wittgenstein 49
   C. Ayer and Positivism 50
   D. "Wittgenstein's Conception of Philosophy" 52

CHAPTER 4

Wittgenstein and His Biographers 59
   A. How Biography Illuminates Language 59
   B. Monk: Life at the Border 69

Preface

It would not have been possible to write the following reflections on Wittgenstein's philosophy except for the publication of Ray Monk's *Ludwig Wittgenstein*.[1] Everyone acquainted with philosophy in this century knows something of Wittgenstein's work and his semi-mysterious existence. Experts offer us appraisals of his technical work, particularly in logic, mathematics, epistemology and language. Writers often start works concerning his thought with a brief biographical chapter. But heretofore these have been rather factual accounts of his wanderings, centering primarily on dates related to the publication of his writing thought. Now Ray Monk has beautifully integrated the "inner struggles" with the outward life, shedding new light on Wittgenstein's unique contribution.

Partly because his professional career began by discussing logic and mathematics with Russell and Frege, there is a tendency to treat Wittgenstein's thought primarily in relationship to his contributions there, which then spilled over into language, the theory of knowledge, and theory of mind. But Monk makes clear that Wittgenstein's own personal relationship to philosophy is far wider than that. In fact, his views about logic and mathematics can be understood as only the first point of attack in a struggle that he has with himself over what philosophy is and does, as well as what role it should play in his own life. The same can be said about religion.

As a lead quote in his study Monk uses a statement by Otto Weininger in *Sex and Character*: "Logic and ethics are fundamentally the same, they are no more than duty to oneself." Given the tormented role which love and sex played in Wittgenstein's life, it is meaningful to see his whole relationship to logic as emerging out of the ethical conflict he had with himself (and later, we will argue, with God) involving the taskmaster role that his sense of duty played in his life and in his work. This is by no means to say that he was clear about what his duty was.

---

[1] Free Press, New York, 1990.

Hamlet-like, as many great figures are, the central struggle, his passion and his energy, arose from the constant unclarity about just what his duty was.

Monk states in his Introduction that "...interest in Wittgenstein... suffers from an unfortunate polarity between those who study his work in isolation from his life and those who find his life fascinating but his work unintelligible."[2] Spiritual and ethical questions dominated his life; rather remote philosophical questions dominated his work. The purpose of the chapters which follow is to work out some of these themes, as they are suggested in Monk's account but not elaborated. This will put Wittgenstein's philosophy in a quite different light, but that is exactly what he himself struggled to do too throughout his lonely life.

Special thanks must go to Dmitry Panasevich and Flora Kidani, who have helped me on a number of projects and who alone are responsible for putting this book into a publishable form. At the start of sabbatical in 1991, the University of Hawaii provided the office space where the complete works of Wittgenstein, Kierkegaard and Tolstoy could be reviewed leisurely. The Pomona College Research Committee provided some funds to help complete the project, and student research assistants have worked on various drafts, Lukas Harris and Bahram Seyedin-Noor.

---

[2] p. xvii-xviii.

1   Philosophical Themes in Wittgenstein's Life

A. Ten Themes

Let me outline a series of themes which dominated Wittgenstein's life, document them from Monk's account, and then, by reviewing his work, show how these can cast his philosophically revolutionary writing in a new light.

(1)   Philosophy as an ascetic practice

Nothing could be greater evidence for Wittgenstein's blend of philosophy with spiritual/ethical concerns than his giving away his considerable fortune and aristocratic status for a life that forced him into dependence on others for his meager needs. This action corresponds to a monk's vow of poverty. The life of philosophy does not itself demand such sacrifice, since it has in its past been compatible with economic and social privilege. The unusual twist which Wittgenstein gave to this situation, as he did to almost his every action, was to give his fortune to his already affluent family, rather than to the poor (as Jesus instructed the rich young ruler to do). He said he did this so that the poor would not be corrupted by money, thus evidencing his still conservative social outlook. His meager meals, often eating the same simple items continuously, his often ragged dress, all testify to his need for a lifestyle appropriate to the seriousness of his work. Philosophy became for him a "religious" way of life, that is, as he would define "religious," meaning not doctrine or ecclesiastical practice but rigor of commitment and action.

(2)   The philosopher as existentialist/pragmatist

We know that Wittgenstein read Kierkegaard and quoted him with approval. We can understand why "the gloomy Dane" attracted him when we see how passionately he felt that philosophy demanded an appropriately severe lifestyle. He read James' *Varieties of Religious Experience* and quotes James with approval too. In this sense he joins the Existentialists and the Pragmatists in their revolt against Hegel and abstract, speculative, historically-based philosophy. Belief is practice; the word is void unless it becomes practice. System-building and any expectation that philosophy can achieve completion are misunderstandings of the human situation, which could only happen due to a detachment of rational thought from its immediate context.

(3) The monk's isolated search for forgiveness

The hermit or the cloistered monk often seem to represent the lifestyle Wittgenstein sought for philosophical as well as spiritual reasons. Wittgenstein had trouble relating to colleagues and continually preferred simple people to sophisticated academics. This set up one of the main tensions and paradoxes he struggled with all his life, since only a very few gifted and trained intellectuals could appreciate his work. Logicians and mathematicians are the epitome of abstracted intellects, and he sought constantly to have a very few gifted students. Yet at the same time he fled the intellectual life to live either in isolation or among simple people.

(4) The penitent's search for forgiveness/salvation

Just as he had a predecessor in Francis of Assisi who also rejected his privileged status, Wittgenstein fought a continual battle with his conscience. As is so often the case with monks in search of a pure life, he seemed unable to forgive himself, felt burdened by his conscience for seemingly insignificant actions or thoughts. He fought the humility vs. pride battle all his life. Could he only have accepted the academic life as his place, pride in his extraordinary intellect might have seemed a virtue. But his constant rejection of academic status and privilege set a brilliant career aside, constantly following Bernard of Clairveaux's search for *The Steps of Humility*.

(5) The struggle with God as an unknown object

Kazanatzakis became physically ill, so intense was his struggle as he poeticized it in *The Saviors of God*. Wittgenstein mirrors the same intensity of struggle without being able to focus on God as its source. His physical energy, if not his health, is drained, but he can never give himself up to belief, much like Simone Weil. He inherits both Judaism and Christianity but can neither appropriate nor reject either or both. He mirrors the feeling in "the hound of heaven," acting as if pursued by God/the Devil and unable to rest or find peace.

(6) Philosophy as a "religious" way of life

Wittgenstein's struggle with philosophy parallels the monk's battle to achieve a pure spiritual life, one free of temptation and guilt. Neither logic nor mathematics in itself dictates such passionate devotion. He quotes Kierkegaard with approval on the need for passion more than reason in one's life. Just as the monk's success in his vocation often produces pride that in turn starts the quest for humility all over again, Wittgenstein gives every evidence in his life and writings of being engaged in an unending struggle, one which he knows cannot end in victory and which will leave him wounded mentally and spiritually.

(7) Philosophy as a life of courage

Although philosophy is a difficult technical subject for many, to see philosophy as a life-pursuit requiring courage is extreme. But for Wittgenstein, philosophy requires courage precisely because its theory, or any theory, is not adequate as a guide to life and may mislead you if taken for truth. Logic in philosophy has the same role that doctrine has in religion. Some people must construct systems and believe in them. They can be instructive and necessary as an enterprise, but if one is seduced by them and does not realize that the only important thing is to live right.

(8) Serious philosophical pursuit has an affinity to mysticism

Contrary to popular opinion, the mystic is not one who utters unintelligible sentences or who resides in unbroken silence. He or she simply knows that words and speech are inadequate to capture truth/reality in any fixed form. But like Wittgenstein, this very impossibility challenges each of us to make the constant attempt, trying endlessly to find words to express a vision. In working constantly to simplify language, in his preference for "ordinary language," one might see Wittgenstein as an empiricist/rationalist. But he seeks to simplify expression and action, as the Zen monk does, because both know that complex verbalization obscures vision by focusing attention on tortuous thought forms.

(9) Language has a mystical quality, if properly seen

The Kabbalist believes that "language in its purest form reflects the fundamental spiritual nature of the world." And so does Wittgenstein. The Kabbalist, the Christian mystic, the Hindu guru, all both fear and explore language, because somewhere within it lies an avenue to truth and enlightenment for the mystic as well as a serious philosophical basis for thought and, for Wittgenstein, an ethical mode of life. A Kabbalist believes speech reaches God because it comes from God. Wittgenstein simplifies speech as a tool for enlightenment.

(10) Insight can be imparted only to one who is serious and dedicated

Although he was an admirer of simple human beings and was often hostile to academic or intellectual pretensions, Wittgenstein was ruthless in not wishing to try to convey his thought to ordinary students. He agreed with Kierkegaard, that to understand an author, the reader must put forward the same intensity of effort that the author did in composing the written work. Being a student requires an appropriately serious style of life. If the student does not combine a rare intellect with an intensity of effort, the power latent in the thought of the teacher will be missed.

Wittgenstein quotes Augustine with admiration, but when it comes to the teacher/student relationship, he could have quoted with approval either Augustine's *Concerning the Teacher* or Plato's *Meno*. The teacher cannot, does not, pour out wisdom. To an unwilling mind nothing can be imparted. Students must teach themselves or never learn. The formal teacher is merely a stimulus, a prod. Anyone can repeat words, thoughts, or a formula. Individual insight is another matter and is more rare. Wittgenstein could quote Augustine: "Who is so stupidly curious as to send his son to school to learn what the teacher thinks?" Philosophical insight has a certain similarity to experiencing unity with God, a rare and overpowering event.

B. BIOGRAPHY AND PHILOSOPHY

How can one interpret Wittgenstein's life and thought, using the themes listed above, when the bulk of the volumes written about him concentrate on the technical aspects of his work. Robert Fogelin's book,[1] for instance, concentrates on the traditional questions, e.g., logical atomism, picturing the world, propositions. He particularly explores the changes from the *Tractatus* to Wittgenstein's later philosophy. All of this can be done in traditional fashion, *a la* a Ph.D. thesis, without mention of Wittgenstein's life, his ethical-religious concerns, or his ambivalence about academic pursuits. "Private" languages and psychology become questions to be argued about in philosophy of mind.

Fogelin does end his book by saying "Wittgenstein's later philosophy is of fundamental importance; it is also radically incomplete" (p. 207). However, to say this seems to suggest that it is up to others to "complete" his task and thus in a sense "solve" the inconsistencies with,

---

[1] *Wittgenstein*, Routledge & Kegan Paul, London, 1976.

or at least radical departures from, the *Tractatus*. But one must ask: (1) what might have caused Wittgenstein to "depart" from the *Tractatus*? It was offered as a "closed system," one that solves philosophical problems with finality. Even though he had great trouble publishing it, and it was little understood, Wittgenstein was convinced that it was a major and definitive work.

As is generally agreed, his whole view of the task of philosophical work underwent a revolution. But in dealing with this, our task is neither that of reconciling Plato's early Socratic dialogues with his later constructive dialogues nor of fitting Hegel's early writings into his later "system." Intent as Wittgenstein was on publishing the *Tractatus*, great hesitation entered into his later writings, so that most were postponed for posthumous printing. Did Wittgenstein see serious technical flaws in the "arguments" of the *Tractatus* (there actually are few arguments; it is more a series of oracular utterances)? But his later writings comment on points in the *Tractatus*, however not very directly; there is no massive analysis.

Criticism from professional colleagues cannot be said to have induced this change. Few understood it enough to say much that was substantive, and Wittgenstein avoided standard academic discussion, substituting instead extended exposition to a few (very few) trusted friends and a very small group of students. Thus, Ray Monk's book does us the service of describing in detail the turbulence and precariousness of Wittgenstein's personal life, which makes Kierkegaard's complaints about his melancholy look like the remarks of a social butterfly (which he was). As befits a monk, Wittgenstein's public life was shaped, finally, to mirror the inner struggle.

Speaking of the later writings in relation to the *Tractatus*, A. M. Quinton remarks: "Wittgenstein's dedication to esotericism both in communication and in the expression of his thoughts, ensured that they would be hard to understand and frequently misunderstood."[2] Logicians, linguistic philosophers, and surely the major thrust of modern philosophy itself, have all aimed at clarity. And Wittgenstein seems to have thought the *Tractatus* would be definitive in its own way. A shift in position is not enough to make one retreat into intentional obscurity. Like Kierkegaard, he seems to have encouraged misunderstanding rather than added clarity.

---

[2] In *Wittgenstein's The Philosophical Investigations*, ed. George Pitcher. University of Notre Dame Press, Notre Dame, 1968, p. 8.

What we perhaps need here is a reference to Nicholas Cusanus' *Learned Ignorance*. Where God is concerned, Nicholas was convinced that the deeper the penetration of our learning (which can be considerable), the more we discover the extent of our final ignorance, a condition which will defy our struggle to overcome it. This is Wittgenstein: increasing our consciousness of difficulties, clarity in language, simplicity in expression, exposing philosophically created puzzles. All this is important, but the whole notion of the possible completeability of our task fades away.

If the *Investigations* changes the view of the *Tractatus* on the relation of language to the world and stresses the impossibility of philosophy, it also adds the same injunction against system building propounded by Nietzsche and Kierkegaard. That is, it is not philosophy's job to propound theories. Considering these restrictions, Quinton remarks: "Historically considered, the two generations of British philosophers who have come under his influence have in effect simply ignored these self-denying ordinances" (p. 10). They excluded clouded utterances in order to make the remainder intelligible, and "they have derived from each of his books a coherent and comprehensive system." (p. 10). But does this not stand Wittgenstein on his head?

It is well known that followers alter their master's instructions even while trying to be faithful. Thus the lament: "I can protect myself well enough against my enemies. God save me from my disciples." All the successors to Socrates claimed allegiance to his outlook and yet were widely varied in their views. Philosophy would be radically different if the young Hegelians had not split into the left and the right. Disciples of Kierkegaard still spend their time trying to establish orthodox interpretations for what he claimed was writing he had so designed as to make that impossible. But is it time to disagree with the "Wittgensteinian right" and argue for his own more radical position?

C. "Vain are the words of the philosopher... if they heal no suffering of man."
—Epictetus

Logicians and philosophers of mathematics have not often tried to use their approach to philosophy to clarify their "life's problems." This is not to say that they have none, but simply to say that these two spheres seldom overlap. Logicians and mathematicians have often been non-normal or even "strange" in their personal behavior, but this was not seen as connected to their technical views. However, from the beginning, with the intensity surrounding the publication of the *Tractatus*, Wittgenstein seemed to place a great deal of weight on achieving finality in philosophy, on the definiteness of his views. This is not connected to the difficulty he had in publishing the volume, since many famous works were either at first rejected or for a time ignored.

Closer to this comes the famous transition in his views and the accompanying doubts about the value of doing or teaching philosophy at all, along with Wittgenstein's personal restlessness about what he should be doing. Logicians change their views, but Wittgenstein's shift seems to involve major upheavals in the very notion of philosophy itself, a fact now much celebrated. What did he want from the *Tractatus*, for himself personally, that was not forthcoming, and how did this change his view of philosophy and dramatically alter his life?—we should ask. Did he expect from logic what logic cannot give?

Wittgenstein's religious interest and the deeply troubling effect of his stringent ethical assessment of life both personal and professional—these are well known. If "you can't get blood out of a turnip," did he expect "solutions" to problems which logic and mathematics cannot provide? To refer to the quote from Epictetus, did he (as only a few philosophers actually do) demand a personal "healing" from intellectual activity which his own approach not only did not allow for but actually blocked? His biography indicates a man concerned with guilt, worried over personal relationships, personally interested in God and religion but unable to commit himself. It is hard to set these aside as outside the scope of his philosophical work, since by his own account it is clear that his philosophy was his life.

Although admittedly not expressed directly, everything about Wittgenstein's intense relationship to his philosophical explorations indicates a man deeply dedicated, if not fiercely aggressive, in wanting philosophy to accomplish great things. To be sure, only a few can do this; it is an esoteric enterprise. But he goes further and demands personal dedication as well as intellectual rigor. The changes in his attitude about, and relationship to, philosophy cannot, it is argued, be explained by the technical problems he encountered in views he held or by changes in evolving views. The process appears more as one of deterioration, personally and in a sense technically, than it does of dialectical progression. Did philosophy prove unable to heal the suffering of man, and is that in fact what he came to demand of it?

2 From the Rigor and Clarity of Logic to the Ineffability and Struggle of the Spirit

What caused the change in the temper, not simply a shift in technical position, from the definiteness of the *Tractatus* to the amorphousness of the *Investigations*? Is there a parallel between this and the rupture of his friendship with Russell and Frege? Others can comment on the change in theoretical position, but the change in style and in outlook is so dramatic as to require explanation. Like the Vienna Circle, the early Wittgenstein was intent on constructing a logical symbolism which obeys the rules of logical grammar (*Tractatus*, 3.325). Thus, it is an ideal language (although later he rejects this) which can be constructed to raise philosophy from its old uncertainties. He cites Russell and Frege, but only remarks that they do not yet "exclude all errors." Evidently, that can be done.

The deepest problems are really *no* problems at all, and philosophy is a "Critique of Language" (4.003-31). One can pin down the pictorial relation which holds between language and the world (4.014). Since the object of philosophy is the logical clarification of thoughts, "it is not a theory but an activity" (4.112). However, this view of philosophy as pragmatic activity depends on the clarity and congruence of the structure of logic and language with reality which Wittgenstein outlined. "Everything that can be said can be said clearly" (4.116). There are the unthinkable and the unspeakable, but philosophy limits these. Does the *Investigations* abandon clarity for an unavoidable venture into the unthinkable? What forced him down this path?

A. The *Tractatus* as a Philosophy of Finality

"The world is completely described by the specification of all elementary propositions plus the specification which of them are true and which are false," of this Wittgenstein is convinced in the *Tractatus* (4.26). Did "another world" open to him, one not subject to such expression, thus forcing him into his dilemma about remaining in academic life? And does this account for why so few, if any, of the students who followed him became logicians/philosophers? Contradictions vanish in the *Tractatus* (5.143); they increasingly appear in and dominate his life after that. In the *Tractatus* the limits of language set the limits of the world (a Vienna Circle project) (5.6); logic filled the world. Later his world seems to have developed "black holes" into which finality disappears. One wonders if Wittgenstein would have taken to "Chaos Theory."

However, in the *Tractatus* Wittgenstein had already concluded that "the sense of the world must lie outside the world," (6.41) in which case there can be no ethical propositions (6.42). In fact, ethics cannot be expressed (6.421). But ethical questions, prominent from the first, increasingly dominate his life. Is it this which renders the structure of the *Investigations* even more esoteric? That world is the mystical (6.44). Yet his optimism is that "if the question can be put at all, then it *can* also be answered" (6.5). The inexpressible is the mystical (6.522), but as Wittgenstein's life is forced into this area, does he lose his ability to put clear questions, which leads in turn to fewer answers and greater obscurity?

As everyone knows, Wittgenstein closes the *Tractatus* by claiming that if one surmounts his propositions, "then he sees the world rightly" (6.54). These propositions are senseless and expendable, but recognizing this is the pinnacle of philosophical clarity. From the mountain top view, he admonishes: "Whereof one cannot speak, thereof one must be silent" (7). (One who has been "enlightened" by Zen practice does not speak about enlightenment.) To invoke the notion of mysticism, the transcendence of the world and the silence it imposes, all this calls up the statements of countless mystics, east and west. Yet, after erecting warnings and barriers, their own experience forces them to try to speak about what is unspeakable. This is what Elie Wiesel tells us about his holocaust experienceexperience in *Night*.

What forced Wittgenstein over the carefully imposed line, thus confounding his followers and unleashing a storm of books and papers all trying to get the untamed tiger back into the cage of logic and clarity? Of course, what seemed personally true to him could have been a personal aberration and thus not applicable to philosophy and to others, except as an occasion for us to launch a clean-up operation. On the other hand, there is good evidence that Wittgenstein's personal life led to his radical change in philosophical outlook. The castle of logic has been erected in all its grandeur, but to borrow from Kierkegaard, Wittgenstein was forced to live in a dog house outside its gates.

B. THE *Investigations* AS THE DE-SYSTEMATIZATION OF PHILOSOPHY

In the preface to the *Investigations*, Wittgenstein stresses its difference in structure. It is "really only an album"[1] (ix). He admits that he jumps from one topic to another, thus abandoning the logical structure of the *Tractatus*. It is, then, like Kierkegaard's *Philosophical Fragments* which self-consciously intends to contrast itself with Hegel's systematic constructions. There are "grave mistakes" (xi) in his first book, he admits, but it was only intended to stimulate others to thought, not to spare people the trouble of thinking. He starts with the quotation from Augustine's *Confessions* about how Augustine learned to use language. But the more telling point may be to ask in what way Wittgenstein increasingly writes his own "confessions."

Primitive language helps clear up the haze which sophisticated use produces. But is there something obscuring in itself which thwarts the simplicity that primitive language use offers? If speaking of "language games" makes language a part of an activity, or a form of life (§23, p. 11), it is possible that this might still lead to unintended complexity, if life itself refuses to become clear but descends into contradiction. Thought is surrounded by a halo; logic presents an order (§97, p. 44). But what is profound resides "in trying to grasp the incomprehensible essence of language" (§97). What has now made language "incomprehensible," when before it was to be the very source of the clarity now possible in thought? There can't be any vagueness in logic, but will that ideal be found in reality (p. 45)?

Examining actual language was once offered as the exercise to end confusion, but now a conflict develops between actual language and our requirement of clarity (§107, p. 46). Since everything lies open to view, philosophy has nothing to explain (§126, p. 50). This may be true for Wittgenstein's writings, but in his life more and more seems to elude his understanding. More and more he seems driven from the public to the private world, something he seeks but in the end fails to enjoy. "The clarity that we are aiming at is indeed *complete* clarity" (§133, p. 52). This is an admirable goal and it means that technical philosophy would

---

[1] *Philosophical Investigations*, trans. G.E.M. Anscombe. Macmillan, New York, 1953.

completely disappear, would become unnecessary. But his life keeps raising tangled "philosophical" puzzles which the clarity of thought does not seem to dispel.

Increasingly, emotions and passions come into consideration; he quotes Kierkegaard on the necessity of passion for belief, not intellect. Philosophy is allowed to find peace because it is no longer tormented by questions which bring itself into question, that ancient first question of philosophy. But if new methods of language have eliminated philosophy's ancient doubt about itself, Wittgenstein himself seems less at peace and more tormented by self doubt. The disparity between his life and his thought heightens and the tension increases. All proceeds tied to the analysis of language in the *Investigations*, until suddenly he remarks: "Language is a labyrinth of paths" (§203, p. 82).

Wittgenstein tells us that "the philosopher's treatment of a question is like the treatment of an illness" (§255, p. 91). This would seem, optimistically, to assume a cure to the illness and leads to the notion of the philosopher as a psychoanalyst. But if the illness is primarily of the spirit, perhaps it is not curable but persistent. §309 introduces the famous phrase: "What is your aim in philosophy? ...To show the fly the way out of the fly bottle" (p. 103). But what if it is the philosopher who has constructed the fly bottle who is himself/herself caught in insoluble ethical/spiritual dilemmas that are problems unlike the releasing of a fly? Teaching is to pass from a piece of disguised nonsense to something that is patent nonsense" (§464, p. 133). But Wittgenstein does not seem to resolve his inner life into patent nonsense. The nonsense remains disguised. To paraphrase Jesus: "Teacher teach thyself."

If "philosophy only states what everyone admits," (§599, p. 156) one begins to think that life's problems are not solved by philosophy, or else we are at odds over our spiritual life and must admit it. Part I of the *Investigations*, although it is more complex and detailed, does not depart far from this optimism about philosophy, except for occasional remarks which seem to hint at skepticism over the possibility of finality. Wittgenstein raises the distinction of "depth grammar" vs. "surface grammar," (§664, p. 168) so that toward the end of Part I it might seem that the *Tractatus* did not run "deep enough" in its exploration of grammar.

Part II moves on to discuss "psychological" concepts, which hardly appear in the *Tractatus*, e.g., feeling, grief, anger. Epistemological problems of perception and philosophy of mind predominate over the intensity of logical rigor. He comments that "religion teaches that the soul can exist when the body has disintegrated" (iv, p. 178) and claims that he can understand this teaching, although he makes it quite clear later that this is different from believing. Still, it is not "nonsense" and he discusses the traditional concept of the soul. But more important for his philosophy's increasing lack of finality, his comment on two "language games" that concern physical objects and sense impression is that there is a complicated relationship between them and "if you try to reduce their relationship to a *simple* formula you go wrong" (§ v, p. 180). We must accept a lack of finality and an absence of resolution.

As is also well known, Wittgenstein became interested in Freud and was not altogether unimpressed. "Dreams" do not quite seem like the logician's subject matter. But something important goes on beneath the surface conscious processes of the rational mind. They yield important information (§xi, p.222), and it becomes important for him to consider this, as Freud did. He returns several times to the "phenomena of belief," (e.g., p. 190) and it seems important to establish a viable meaning. But he remarks obscurely, "Do not try to analyze your own inner experience," (§xi, p. 204) which at least suggests that this exists just as much as mathematical calculations and public action.

Aesthetic experience enters as important (§xi, p. 219). And he shows an increasing affinity with Pragmatism when he remarks: "Let the use of words teach you their meaning" (§xi, p. 220). What is *internal* is hidden from us. The future is also hidden from us (p. 223). Existentialists speak about the future as important, logicians seldom. And he returns to the notion, like Marx, of action: "Ask not: "What goes on in us when we are certain that...?" [a question of philosophy of mind—but: how is "the certainty that is the case" manifested in human action?]" (p. 225). Life becomes our subject: "What has to be accepted, the given, is... *forms of life*" (p. 226). Even mathematics is active: "In one sense mathematics is a branch of knowledge—but still it is also an *activity*" (p. 227).

"Learning" and "teaching" are important to Wittgenstein, even as he increasingly shies away from them as being professionally barren. "What one acquires here is not a technique; one learns correct judgments. There are also rules, but they do not form a system, and any experienced person can apply them right. Unlike calculation rules, what is most difficult here is to put this indefiniteness, correctly and unfalsified, into words" (p. 227). Style of implementation is important and an ultimate indefiniteness, not clarity, underlies words. Then, should we be interested "not in grammar but rather in the nature which is the basis of grammar" (p. 230)? Philosophy has emerged from language study as a source of clarity and returned to nature and indefiniteness.

C. PHILOSOPHY AS DETACHED UTTERANCE: THE BLUE & THE BROWN BOOKS

These writings are considered as "preliminary studies" for the *Investigations*, but they have a special quality about them which is important to Wittgenstein's radically changing views on philosophy as an enterprise. They are sets of notes dictated to his classes, restricted in circulation, vs. the *Tractatus*, and they are esoteric in quality. "They are meant for the people who heard the lectures," he cautions (Preface, p. v).[2] Philosophy is still a method of investigating puzzles, but his conception of the method was changing, Russell reports. Understanding is not one thing (as it might be for logic); it is as various as the language games themselves. This involves the study of primitive forms of language or primitive languages. The mental mist surrounding our ordinary use of language then disappears, he hopes.

Logic was supposed to govern the unity of language; but language, as we use it, does not have that kind of unity, Russell comments in his Preface. But why did Wittgenstein find that the generality he desired along with other philosophers, and the conclusiveness in deciding philosophical questions he shared with the Vienna Circle, had not come from the *Tractatus*? Was the shift to the study of language brought about because the language of the *Tractatus* proved as much "mystical" as conclusive, thus frustrating his own intensity to find his life's meaning and satisfaction in formal philosophy? Philosophy cannot be like a science, he concludes (p. 18).

But perhaps more important, Wittgenstein's interest is shifting away from the "craving for generality," (p. 18) which he attributes to philosophers as a failing, and he decries their (his former) "contemptuous attitude toward the particular case" (p. 18). And here we might pause and consider his reading of Kierkegaard as a source of insight. Søren Kierkegaard had rebelled against Hegel's abstract generality and wanted his tombstone marked with what he considered his prime concentration: "The Individual" (this was not done). Existentialism argues that particular persons, situations, and cases require specific and individual consideration and decision, which cannot come from the universal. Wittgenstein departs from the formal

---

[2] *The Blue & Brown Books*, Basil Blackwell, Oxford, 1958.

universality of logic and mathematics and focuses on individuals and, in his case, individual utterances.

Philosophy, he states, is "a fight against the fascination which forms of expression exert upon us" (p. 27). Kierkegaard could have said the same about Hegel whom he thought had become captured by the word-systems we build and ignored the individuals who have problems unresolved by printed theories. We give our words meaning (p. 28) and so should not be enchanted by their sound. He denies that he is looking for an ideal language; "ordinary language is all right" (p. 28). But we must try to counteract the misleading effect of certain analogies. We do not accept ordinary language uncritically, either. His is a "new" philosophical approach, but it is an heir to old philosophies.

He begins to talk more about individual experience. He was interested in this but postponed consideration because "thinking about the topic raises a host of philosophical difficulties which threaten to break up all our commonsense notions about what we should commonly call the objects of our experience" (p. 44). The *Tractatus* was not an end in itself but rather abstractions aimed at clearing the ground, as its ending states. "No philosophical problem can be solved until all philosophical problems are solved," (p. 44) so that logic and mathematics (even metaphysics) cannot stand alone or make sense alone or be judged alone. He has now taken up new problems (particular experience), and "every new problem which arises may put in question the position which our previous partial results are to occupy in the final picture" (p. 44).

The *Brown Book* opens with the now well known quote from Augustine, whom Wittgenstein admires. Augustine's view of learning names is adequate as a starting point, he feels. Mental acts, meaning, color, language games, primitive languages now occupy Wittgenstein's time. Feelings are given prime consideration. The topics move from mathematics and logic to psychology. The ladder of the *Tractatus* did get us there, but it proves its own uselessness if we want to go further, as he said. The past, the present, and the future have problematic and almost mysterious aspects (p. 107). Logic is not temporal and so the mystery of time arises only "at the limit of logic."

Like Nietzsche and Kierkegaard, the future also becomes a problem which neither the historical past nor timeless truths can help us deal with. "The idea of a proposition saying something about what will happen in the future is even more liable to puzzle us than the idea of a proposition about the past" (p. 109). Kierkegaard had said the same.

Thinking about the future brings logic up against an ultimate contingency and uncertainty. Wittgenstein claims that his method is "purely descriptive," with not even hints of explanations (p. 125). Is this because statements about human psychology and the future are not subject to "explanations" as the past and logic may be? He takes over the puzzle of time's passage from Augustine and, as with Kierkegaard, it cannot be reduced to logic.

"The problem we are concerned with we also encounter in thinking about volition, deliberate and involuntary action" (p. 150). The art of working puzzles has now become Wittgenstein's preoccupation, not the finality in the *Tractatus* (which proved impossible; remember, it only led beyond itself). If as G.E. Moore remarked, following Wittgenstein "required a "sort of thinking" to which we are not accustomed and to which we have not been trained,"[3] surely the *Tractatus*, for all its novel suggestion, is an old form of thought which can be discussed on conventional grounds. What has now led Wittgenstein beyond the limits of formal language, toward ordinary language, unorthodox procedures, and less solvable problems?

D. Certainty and Religion

Propositions which come back again and again, "as if bewitched," Wittgenstein would like to expunge from philosophical language.[4] He begins his quest for certainty in logic and mathematics, but in classical thought, such recurrences were taken to be the "perennial" problems of philosophy, subjects for concentration not banishment. Yet he is not unwilling to let Catholics say that Jesus had only a human mother. It is just that they must add, "I believe" not "I know" this (p. 32e). "Knowledge" and "certainty" belong to two different categories (p. 39e). Very intelligent and well educated people believe in the story of creation in the Bible, he admits (p. 43e). "My life consists in my being content to accept many things" (p. 44e).

Wittgenstein sees that he seeks knowledge "under the aspect of eternity," as Spinoza put it. "Is God bound by our knowledge? Are a lot of our statements *incapable* of falsehood? For that is what we want to say" (p. 57e). "There are cases where doubt is unreasonable, but others where it seems logically impossible. And there seems to be no clear boundary between them. Do I want to say, then, that certainty resides

---

[3] "Wittgenstein's Lectures in 1930-33," *Mind*, vol. I, LXIV, January, 1955, No. 253, p. 26.

[4] *On Certainty*, trans. Paul & Anscombe. Basil Blackwell, Oxford, 1969, p. 6.

within language games?" (p. 59e). Wittgenstein began by yearning for certainty but reverses this as he moves along.

Frazer's *Golden Bough* became popular, but it might be thought not to be anything of interest to Wittgenstein. It was taken as a "defense" of religious belief, showing to a scientific age the continued fascination of religion. Of course, Wittgenstein was increasingly disenchanted with science as a model for philosophy. In the beginning of his commentary on Frazer[5] his statement is "we must find the road from error to truth," but he adds: "I must plunge again and again into the waters of doubt" (p. 1e). What he finds in Frazer is what strikes him as "terrible, impressive, horrible, tragic, etc., anything but trivial and insignificant, that is what gives birth to them" (p. 3e).

Then he moves on to say: "We can only describe and say, human life is like that" (p. 3e). How different this is from the world of logic/mathematics. But it attracted Wittgenstein and he thought it "not different in kind from any genuinely religious action today, say a confession of sins" (p. 4e). There is a mistake only if magic is presented as science, and we know Wittgenstein to have been absorbed with the notion of sin and confession. Any phenomenon can become mysterious for us, "and it is precisely the characteristic of the awakening human spirit that a phenomenon has meaning for it" (p. 7e).

His fascination with Frazer's account of savage religious belief leads Wittgenstein to one of his anti-English remarks, sounding almost like Nietzsche: "...these savages will not be so far from my understanding of spiritual matters as an Englishman of the twentieth century" (p. 8e). And then sounding like C.G. Jung he comments that "whole mythology is deposited in our language" (p. 10). We cannot pass by such a comment lightly, since we know Wittgenstein's feeling about our languages as the field of inquiry and one where philosophy finds what "solutions" as are possible. Thus, the whole mythology of savage religious practice is not long gone but is present still in the language we analyze.

We are all well aware of Wittgenstein's interest in psychology and his remarks on color, but not as much attention has been paid to his brief *Lectures & Conversations on Aesthetics, Psychology and Religious Belief.*[6] In discussing Freud he comments: "Suppose you look on

---

[5] *Remarks on Frazer's Golden Bough*, trans. A.C, Miles and Rush Rhees, Brynmill Press, Nottinghamshire, 1979.
[6] Notes edited by Cyril Barrett, University of California Press, Berkeley, 1967.

a dream as a kind of language" (p. 48). Like the primitive mythology still resident in language, this thought fits very nicely into Freud's theory, a thinker whom we might not have thought would interest Wittgenstein seriously.

Dreams are ways of symbolizing something. And we need next to find a way of translating this symbolism into the language of ordinary speech. Freud's belief in the unconscious did not in itself deter Wittgenstein, since Freud also believed in the rational translatability out of the unconscious via dream analysis. It is probably correct to reject the idea that Wittgenstein thought of himself as translating psychoanalytic teaching into philosophy, as has been suggested, but his acceptance of dreams as of symbolic importance is significant, although Wittgenstein is not sure that dreaming is a language at all.

In "Lectures on Religious Belief" Wittgenstein asks if he could say he does not believe in a "Judgment Day." Should he say he does not believe that there will be such a thing? He replies: "It would seem to me utterly crazy to say this" (p. 55). He believes that, in religious discourse, we use such expressions as "I believe" in ways utterly different from the way in which we use them in science (p. 57). When it comes to "God," Wittgenstein acknowledges that it is among the earliest words we learn. And if "the question arises of the existence of a god or God, it plays an entirely different role to that of the existence of any person or object I ever heard of," (p.59) he concludes with a remark quite similar to St. Anselm's view.

Wittgenstein likes Michelangelo's Sistine Chapel ceiling with its picture of God creating man, since "there is nothing which explains the meaning of words as well as a picture" (p. 63). It is interesting that in so difficult a concept as creation Wittgenstein finds a picture to be as good evidence as is possible. "Unshakable belief" will be shown, not by reason or evidence, but by "regulating life" (p. 54). Practical application is his test of belief, as it is for William James. Speaking of reading the Epistles, he comments: "Not only is it not reasonable, but it doesn't pretend to be" (p. 58). About belief, he remarks: "One should *do* something" (p. 69).

Is Wittgenstein trying to undermine reason, he asks, and he responds: "This wouldn't be false. This is actually where such questions arise" (p. 69). Asked if he knows whether he will survive death, he would say "I can't say 'I don't know' because I haven't any clear idea what I'm saying when I'm saying 'I don't cease to exist,' etc." (p. 70). To say more is to be philosophically arrogant (p. 72). So as Hume points out, the skeptic and the believer are not far apart and both are contrasted to the dogmatism or the atheist. They both claim to know, and the believer ought not to do so. We ought not to reject what we recognize that transcends our ability to finalize, since that assumes finalities. But we should acknowledge the limits of our understanding.

E. PHILOSOPHY IN A WIDER CONTEXT

Perhaps the bulk of Wittgenstein's written work concerns logic, mathematics, his changing concept of philosophy itself, or, in the later years, philosophy of mind and psychology (more properly, psychological remarks). In editing *Culture and Value*, G.H. von Wright tells us that he decided not to eliminate much of these remarks left in Wittgenstein's notes. Some are "beautiful and profound"[7] (Foreword), he remarks. These "extra-philosophical" writings in fact set off Wittgenstein's core philosophy in an enlightening way. So much of his writing is aphoristic or oracular in style, and since he went through obvious changes of mind, the reader's first task should be to try to set the whole enterprise in a wider context.

Early on (1929), Wittgenstein makes clear that mathematics is not his model for philosophy (perhaps this is why he could not join the Vienna Circle). "There is no religious denomination in which the misuse of metaphysical expression has been responsible for so much sin as it has in mathematics" (p. 1e). Nor is "nature" his model and limits. "What is good is also divine. Queer as it sounds, that sums up my ethics. Only something supernatural can express the supernatural" (p. 3e). And it is not the case that, as years pass, he rejects such comments. Religious/ethical issues persist throughout, although he is no Kierkegaard in constant religious concentration.

One can of course take the "bulk" of Wittgenstein's philosophical writing and sift it to find "conclusions." But this does not account for the constant upheaval in his life, for the "strange" style of his increasingly unsystematic writing, and particularly not for his own "unhappiness" with formal philosophical work. One can consider problems in math, logic, language and psychology, as he did, and leave them on their own. But since Wittgenstein did not do that, the reader who does may risk missing the driving force behind the almost chaotic production and his distressed existence. One can imagine that he would have approved of a remark by Kierkegaard: that a reader who wishes to understand an

---

[7] trans. Peter Winch, University of Chicago Press, Chicago, 1980.

author must put forward the same amount of passion and effort in attending that the writer did in formulating his phrases.

There is a way, he tells us (1930), of capturing the world sub specie aeterni through the work of the artist (he liked artistic, musical examples, and he was himself skilled musically). "Thought has such a way—so I believe—it is as though it flies above the world and leaves it as it is—observing it from above, in flight" (p. 5e). "Man must awake to wonder"; science is a way of putting him to sleep (p. 5e). His philosophy is unpoetic and heads for what is concrete. Things are not covered by any veil. "This is where religion and art part company" (p. 6c). "Each sentence I write is trying to say the whole thing" (p. 7e). He reads Lessing on the Bible: it is a great temptation to try to make the spirit explicit.

Except for the *Tractatus*, Wittgenstein would seem to be anti-Hegelian, anti-systematic, much like Kierkegaard, James, and Nietzsche. And yet he remarks (1931): "A thinker is very much like a draughtsman whose aim is to represent all the interrelations between things," (p. 12e) which is not unlike either Hegel or British idealism. Of course, one could suggest that this remained Wittgenstein's deepest wish but that his rejection of the finality of logic and mathematics left him without a base. He was definitely anti-progress where human problems are concerned; no dialectic animates his works. These are fragments, momentary insights, as Kierkegaard might say, or thoughts out of season, as Nietzsche might say, no matter how much cleaning up and systematization his followers have done. Perhaps that is why he feared for his students. "What you have achieved cannot mean more to others than it does to you. Whatever it has cost you, that's what they will pay" (p. 14c). And followers tend to simplify; it is the student's first task in an attempt to understand profundity.

Christianity has God say: "Don't act a tragedy, that's to say, don't enact heaven and hell on earth. Heaven and hell are my affairs" (p. 14c). Just as Jesus was not orthodox in his time, Wittgenstein was not. Yet it is odd how many have missed the religious themes that appear constantly in his biography and which emerge in his writing as well. What is the relationship of his constant struggle with religious issues, guilt, forgiveness, God, and his larger philosophical work? With Kierkegaard this is obvious and he read Kierkegaard. But Wittgenstein's start in logic did not allow this to come through clearly—at first.

In discussing the lack of "progress" in philosophy, Wittgenstein comments (1931): "It is because our language has remained the same and keeps seducing us into asking the same questions" (p. 15e). If we stare at something no explanation seems capable of clearing it up, as he suggests. But it could be that "life" continuously presents the same problems, which our language simply reflects, not that language itself is the origin. If we have come up against the limits of human understanding, we think we can see beyond them, which satisfies a longing for the transcendent. To paraphrase "Socratic ignorance": in order to know that you do not know you need to know quite a bit.

And he throws considerable light on the famous ending of the *Tractatus* concerning silence and the inexpressible: "Perhaps what is inexpressible (what I find mysterious and am not able to express) is the background against which whatever I could express has its meaning" (p. 16e). Working in philosophy is like working on oneself; it tests the limits of our ignorance. Importance comes from what everyone can understand (he says quoting Tolstoy), but "...the very things which are the most obvious may become the hardest to understand. What has to be overcome is a difficulty having to do with the will, rather than the intellect" (p. 17e). As it was for Kierkegaard, decision is the main block to human understanding, or that is, of our failure to reach one.

Although formally Christian, Wittgenstein is in touch with his "Jewishness." "Amongst Jews 'genius' is found only in the holy man. Even the greatest Jewish thinker is no more than talented (myself for instance)" (p. 18e). "It is typical of the Jewish mind to understand someone else's work better than he understands himself" (p. 19e). There is much in Wittgenstein's biography to suggest that he sought, or at least admired, the holy man's life. He remarks on the necessity of courage, else philosophy become just a clever game. His isolated style of existence is connected to Jewish "secretiveness." Jews continue to exist despite persecution "only because they have an inclination toward such secretiveness" (p. 22e).

Evidencing his love for music, he says: "Philosophy ought to be written only as a poetic composition" (p. 24c, 1933). He evidences the monk's zeal for an ideal of perfection by adding: I thereby reveal myself "as someone who cannot quite do what he would like to be able to do" (p. 24c, 1933). He sought conclusiveness in philosophy, and for a time he claimed its achievement, but now (1934-6) he sees its resemblance to aesthetics. It is wishful thinking to prophesy that the next generation will solve these problems (p. 25e). He has come around to agree with Plato, Kierkegaard, Nietzsche, etc. about the necessary inconclusiveness of the philosophical quest, all the while expounding on a method to "resolve" philosophical problems.

Few were more fierce than Wittgenstein in being sure of his philosophical genius. Yet the paradox: "The edifice of your pride has to be dismantled. And that is terribly hard work" (p. 26e). (The novice master tells the novice monk the same thing). Hard on others, he was equally hard on himself, as is true of the monastic pursuit. Philosophy easily degenerates into dogmatism. The only way to guard against distortion in our assertions is to remember that the ideal to which we appeal is merely a yardstick, an object of comparison (p. 26e). Plato of course makes the same statement about the ideal Republic or the form of the Good. Ideals, thus, are not attainable and are not intended as such, but they still exist as models to which we compare our work.

Wittgenstein is famed for a new method of doing philosophy connected to analyzing language. But when one considers the furious inner struggle which characterizes his life until the end, it is instructive to consider him as a pragmatist/existentialist: "The way to solve the problem you see in life is to live in a way that will make what is problematic disappear" (p. 27e). His purist sense of ethics haunts his every action, and his unhappiness with any lifestyle becomes understandable when this is seen against the furious effort he poured into trying to find the mode of existence that would solve problems—from giving away his fortune to isolating himself in a hut in Norway, to voluntarily fighting as a common soldier exposed to danger.

The analysis of language games, exploring primitive or ordinary language, did nothing to resolve Wittgenstein's life problems. Theories do not do it. He learns this from his acute understanding of Christianity. It is not a doctrine. It is a description of something that actually takes place in human life. "For "consciousness of sin" is a real event and so are despair and salvation through faith" (p. 28e). Wittgenstein seems constantly to seek forgiveness, and, like Sartre, it is all the harder to achieve since he does not have a God to grant this. Despair is evident in his nearness to suicide, but it is salvation through faith that he never experiences, although he seems to understand it and never to deny its possibility.

Tension, contrast, paradox is everywhere. That is why to systematize Wittgenstein into clarity is to miss so much that is real. "Forcing my thoughts into an ordered sequence is a torment for me," he reports (p. 28e), and everyone who attended his "lectures" (his thought sessions) would agree. "Religious similes can be said to move on the edge of an abyss," (p. 29e) as Kierkegaard and Sartre remarked too. He seems to have been led by his own life close to an abyss. Yet he preferred the simplicity, the humility of the Gospels to Paul's pride and anger, insisting first on his own person (p. 30e). And there is something revealing here about the tension in Wittgenstein's own life. Pride, complexity, self-awareness were his life, and yet there seems to be a constant yearning for simplicity, humility. The unresolvable contradiction he denied to mathematics appears in life.

"Language —I want to say—is a refinement, in the beginning was the deed," (p. 31e) quoting Goethe. Thus to restrict Wittgenstein to language games is to miss his intensity about action. Is Scripture unclear? Can it be clarified by linguistic analysis as scholars have tried? He responds: "If we want to warn someone of a terrible danger, do we go about it by telling him a riddle whose solution will be the warning?" (p. 31e). What you are supposed to see cannot be communicated even by the best and most accurate historians. So there are "terrible dangers" in life about which Christianity constitutes a warning. This is not easy to see, and insisting on clarity is itself a distortion.

If you are to believe Christianity, you can only do this as the result of a life (e.g., the narratives of Jesus). If the accounts of the Gospels were historically false, belief might still lose nothing by this (p. 32e). The message of the Gospels is seized on by men believingly, lovingly. Wittgenstein echoes Kierkegaard on the misunderstanding of Christianity in the historical approach. His "seized on by men believingly" is like Kierkegaard's "leap of faith" (a step which he, Wittgenstein, never took). "That is the certainty characterizing the particular acceptance-as-true, not something else" (p. 32e). But Wittgenstein does not claim this for himself; he only seems to admire it, perhaps even to miss it in his own life. "I cannot utter the word 'Lord' with meaning." "And it could say something to me, only if I lived *completely* differently" (p. 33e).

"You cannot write anything about yourself that is more truthful than you yourself are" (p. 33e). As the monk strives for purity and perfection, Wittgenstein did in philosophy. Yet as it became clear that goal could not be achieved, the pressure increased in his lifestyle. "So we have to content ourselves with wisdom and speculation. We are in a sort of hell where we can do nothing but dream, roofed in, as it were, and cut off from heaven. But if I am to be *really* saved—what I need is *certainty*—not wisdom, dreams or speculations—and this certainty is faith. And faith is faith in what is needed by my heart, my soul, not my speculative intelligence" (p. 33e, 1937). Pascal could say it no better.

This is a revealing comment, an amazing one for a logician, or perhaps we should say: these are words only a logician could form whose life was not satisfied with numbers, theories, words. "For it is my soul with its passions, as it were its flesh and blood, that has to be saved, not my abstract mind." "So this can come about only if you no longer rest your weight on earth but suspend yourself from heaven" (p. 33e, 1937). Doubt can be combated only by redemption. Wittgenstein's life can be seen as one constantly pressing for redemption but never experiencing it—and being so fiercely honest that he could neither give up what he desired nor fake what he had not experienced.

However, honesty often comes at a high price: "Nothing is as difficult as not deceiving oneself," (p. 34e) he remarks in a passage echoing Sartre's "self-deception." Longfellow's words, "for the gods are everywhere" could serve him as a motto, Wittgenstein claimed (p. 34e). His life is almost as forced by internal pressure as Kazanatzakis' search for God. "The measure of genius is character," (p. 35e) not brilliance in theory. And Wittgenstein neither relaxed in his personal life nor in self-searching. "Within all great art there is a WILD animal *tamed*" (p. 37e). "Aim at being loved without being admired," (p. 38e) he states. And yet the irony is that love was in short supply in his life while admiration abounded. Perhaps that is why he fled the limelight constantly, seeking love—but in isolation.

The creator built wonderful laws into numbers (p. 41e, 1942). Yet they do not satisfy the longing soul. "If you already have a person's love no sacrifice can be too much to give for it; but any sacrifice is too great to buy it for you" (p. 42e) (c.f. Jesus: "For what shall it profit a man..."). This is ironic, since Wittgenstein sacrificed little for love and yet constantly seems to have been in need. He sought it, but did he know how to give it? "A philosopher is a man who has to cure many intellectual diseases in himself before he can arrive at the notion of common sense" (p. 44e). Wittgenstein behaved very much like a great believer in common sense, but also as one who fought continually to cure himself.

"A miracle is, as it were, a *gesture* which God makes" (p. 45e, 1944). "Now do I believe this happens? I don't" (p. 45e, 1944). But he does not rule it out. He only states it has not happened to him. "Go on, believe! It does no harm," he adds. Believing means submitting to authority, something genius does not do easily. But a religious man thinks himself wretched, although any half-way decent man "will think himself extremely imperfect" (p. 45e, 1944).

Wittgenstein's life seems to have been burdened by his intense effort for perfection (philosophy as an ascetic practice) and by feelings of being wretched (thoughts of suicide). "The Christian religion is only for the man who needs infinite help, solely, that is, for the man who experiences infinite torment" (p. 46e). "Words are deeds."

"And my conceit of being an extraordinary person has been with me *much* longer than my awareness of my particular talent" (p. 47e, 1946). This is contrasted with: "And only if I were able to submerge myself in religion could these doubts be stilled [logic had not done it]. Because only religion would have the power to destroy vanity and penetrate all the nooks and crannies" (p. 48e). He comments: "In former times people went into monasteries" (p. 49e). Such measures were taken because the problems were difficult. Wittgenstein could only flee into isolation, resign distinguished professorships and consider monkhood.

Again and again Wittgenstein shows his approach to religion as a practical activity and not an intellectual enterprise. "The way you use the word "God" does not show *whom* you mean—but rather what you mean" (p. 50e). "I believe that one of the things Christianity says is that sound doctrines are all useless. That you have to change your life" (p. 53e). As one who did change circumstances repeatedly he remarks: "If life becomes hard to bear, we think of a change in our circumstances. But the more important and effective change, a change in our own attitude, hardly ever occurs to us" (p. 53e). "Here you need something to move you and turn you in a new direction" (p. 53e). Then the man of supreme intellect comments: "Wisdom is passionless. But faith by contrast is what Kierkegaard calls a *passion*" (p. 53e).

Wittgenstein can be said to have sought a radical turn in his life, conversion in the religious sense, salvation (or forgiveness) in the secular sense, but it is clear that he never achieved/experienced this. "I am often afraid of madness," he reports (p. 53e). Loneliness and isolation spark this feeling, but Wittgenstein cultivates this at the same time that he protests it. He reflects: "Is it that I *will* not open my heart to anyone anymore, or that I cannot?" (p. 54e, 1946). "I cannot kneel to pray because it's as though my knees were stiff" (p. 56e). "Wisdom is cold and to that extent stupid" (p. 56e).

But should not the fame of his work console him? Others would bask in it. "Is what I am doing really worth the effort? Yes, but only if a higher light shines on it from above" (p. 57e). "Only people who hold you in esteem and at the same time *love* you can make it easy for you to behave like this" (p. 58e). That Wittgenstein sought love (and made it difficult to be given) is clear; that he gave love is not so clear. Like Kierkegaard, he dreaded followers and establishing "a school." "I cannot found a school because I do not really want to be imitated" (p. 61e). "I am by no means sure that I should prefer a continuation of my work by others to a change in the way people live which would make all these questions superfluous" (p. 61e). "Vain are the words of the philosopher..."?

Again the pragmatic/existentialist theme: "It strikes me that a religious belief could only be something like a passionate commitment to a system of reference. Hence, although it's *belief*, it's really a way of living..." (p. 64e). Wittgenstein had a clear idea of what was needed but, it appears, never the commitment. Perhaps his intellect was too intense to allow it, although it could state the goal. Nothingness is instructive to one who can stand it, as Sartre said. "When you are philosophizing you have to descend into primeval chaos and feel at home there" (p. 65e). "Industry like that requires humility and an enormous capacity for suffering, hence strength" (p. 71e).

There is never a hint but that Wittgenstein had respect, or even admiration, for sincere religious believers. "An honest religious thinker is like a tight-rope walker. He almost looks as though he were walking on nothing but air. His support is the slenderest imaginable. And yet it really is possible to walk on it" (p. 73e, 1948). Perhaps it is Kierkegaard's honesty and passion which attracted Wittgenstein. Yet like Moses, Wittgenstein could lead us up to, but was not allowed to enter, the promised land. "Man's greatest happiness is love," (p. 77e) he repeats. Yet he seems unable to transfer that into deed. "What is eternal and important is often hidden from a man by an impenetrable veil" (p. 80e). And so it seems that it was for him.

"If Christianity is the truth then all the philosophy that is written about it is false" (p. 83e). Evidence-by-practice-in-life ("By their fruits they shall be known.") returns as a theme again and again, and it comes from a man intently bound up in the cerebral life. "How do I know that these people mean the same when each says he believes in God?" (p. 85e). "Practice gives the words their sense" (p. 85e). "Perhaps someone could convince someone that "God exists" by means of a certain kind of upbringing, by shaping his life in such and such a way" (p. 85e). "So if you want to stay within the religious sphere you must *struggle*," (p. 86e) says Wittgenstein, a man who struggled with himself and his mind all his life, just as Kierkegaard did. But both produced valuable writings by damaging themselves in the process.

F. SOPHISTICATED TRIVIALIZING

Wittgenstein began by dealing with the whole scope of philosophy, taking on its widest range. In his personal life we know that he increasingly agonized over ethical/religious themes and drove himself more and more into isolation and ascetic rigors, all the while longing for love, forgiveness, and justification. Why, then (except for the private remarks) does the bulk of his written work become more a series of individual comments and dwell extraordinarily on color, on perception, and on states of mind, e.g., feeling. His developed method for doing philosophical work need not turn him away from the central concerns of life but rather could lead him to clarify them.

The Foreword to *Philosophical Remarks*[8] reads as if it could have been written by Augustine for the *Confessions*. "I would like to say 'This book is written to the glory of God,' but nowadays that... would not be rightly understood. It means the book is written in good will, and in so far as it is not so written, but out of vanity, etc., the author would wish to see it condemned. He cannot free it of its impurities further than he himself is free of them" (p. 7). Here we see the harsh self-judgment, the striving for the pure, the ascetic life, that characterized so much of Wittgenstein's days. But the book itself is full of miscellaneous abstractions, only occasionally broken into by important remarks.

"The complexity of philosophy is not in its matter, but in our tangled understanding," he begins (p. 9). Yet, he perfects a method for untangling our understanding all the while his life grows more complex. So: is "philosophy" concerned with personal life or not? "How strange," he says, "if logic were concerned with an 'ideal' language, and not with *ours!*" (p. 9). Wittgenstein began by wanting finality in philosophy and flirted with the Vienna Circle's notion of an ideal language. But in rejecting both did he really go to *"ours,"* the language of the people? Are most of the examples of language used of the kind which concern humanity at large, or is it about the "logical puzzles" of grammar? We cannot exclude the element of "intention" from language (p. 11), he reports, but what do most people "intend" when they speak?

Wittgenstein notes: "The moment we try to apply exact concepts of measurement to immediate experience, we come up against a particular

---

[8] Ed. Rush Rhees, trans. R. Hargrave & R. White, University of Chicago Press, Chicago, 1975.

vagueness in this experience" (p. 40). "Analyzing the grammar of speech" and "coming up against immediate experience," then, cannot be the same thing. Clarity comes in technical structures: "A proposition is completely analyzed if its grammar is made completely clear" (p. 51). His frustration comes out: "Why is philosophy so complicated? It ought, after all to be completely simple" (p. 52). Yet still he clings to the hope: "Although the *result* of philosophy is simple, its methods for arriving there cannot be so" (p. 52). Responding to this we can only ask: were the results of Wittgenstein's philosophy really "simple," even on his own account?

He knows that strictly linguistic symbols form only a small part of ordinary thought process (p. 54). As Augustine said: all words are signs but not all signs are words. So then, can the analysis of language exhaust the thought process? "Time and again the attempt is made to use language to limit the world and set it in relief—but it can't be done. The self-evidence of the world expresses itself in the very fact that language can and does only refer to it" (p. 80). Thus, the analysis of language cannot solve our problems about "the world," because language does not contain our world but only refers to it, symbolizes it. "What belongs to the essence of the world cannot be expressed by language" (p. 84).

However, the confidence of the grammarian of logic returns: "But the essence of language is a picture of the essence of the world; and philosophy as custodian of grammar can in fact grasp the essence of the world" (p. 85). Heidegger might have said that—or a Kabbalist; (see later). Still: if we can grasp the essence of the world through grammar, is that the same as to understand or, more important, to comprehend the world? Although it is in our "grasp," does the world in any way still remain closed or secret? He adds: "What we understand by the word "language" unwinds in physical time" (p. 98). This sounds innocent enough, until we remember his quoting Augustine on the problem of time and agreeing that time involves properties which block understanding.

"In philosophy it's always a matter of the application of a series of utterly simple basic principles that any child knows, and the enormous difficulty is only one of applying these in the confusion our language creates" (p. 153). To which we respond: but what about the world distinct from language? And Wittgenstein does back away from the childlike simplicity of philosophy: "But the difficulty in applying the simple basic principles shakes our confidence in the principles themselves" (p. 154). Then, is it language which proves not to be so simply reducible, or is it the world over against it which frustrates the application of our simple principles?

Why does Wittgenstein's writing become consciously a series of sometimes not connected remarks? Like Kierkegaard, he denies the possibility of constructing a system in philosophy. "Therefore, we can't search for a system: what we *can* search for is the expression for a system that is given to me in unwritten symbols" (p. 178). Can we perfectly translate the "unwritten" symbols into verbal form? Wittgenstein uses the example of a school boy's elementary trigonometry problem, and he thinks the boy can. But are the world and life so easily translatable into written form, or is mathematics a poor example where our ability to express life and the world is concerned? "There are no gaps in mathematics," Wittgenstein reports (p. 187). But should that all the more make us question mathematics as a model for understanding our world which is full of gaps. "Mathematics cannot be incomplete" (p. 188).

But in his oscillation between complete clarity and finality and then denying its possibility, Wittgenstein goes back to his belief in grammatical clarity: "Whatever I can understand, I must completely understand" (p. 188). Logical analysis does not have to add anything to arrive at complete clarity. Yet: "...even the most unclear seeming proposition retains it previous content intact after the analysis and all that appears is that its grammar is made clear" (p. 188). Oddly, this leaves open the possibility that our analysis makes grammatical structure perfectly clear, just as desired, but that the content of the proposition which caused our original unclarity might not itself be "fully cleared up" by grammatical analysis.

"A number must measure" (p. 230). But is our world exhaustively measured by number, as Pythagoras once thought and logicians still often do? "If inconsistencies were to arise between the rules of the game of mathematics, it would be the easiest thing in the world to remedy" (p. 319). You make a new stipulation to cover the case in which the rules conflict. But is that a good analogy for the inconsistencies in life and in our philosophies about life? Can these be treated as a game in which we change the rules by stipulation? Mathematicians find contradiction to be a nightmare. Wittgenstein does not share this fear. Still, if we should not worry about contradictions in mathematics, do these appear in our experience in ways not so easily solved?

The editors of *Philosophical Remarks*[9] have intentionally selected comments from Wittgenstein's posthumous writings that are of a "philosophical" nature. But as we proceed through the rest of the later writings, how much do they concern themselves with crucial and agonizing philosophical questions? The *Philosophical Grammar* takes up issues central to Wittgenstein's concern for insight into language or into philosophy. *Philosophical Remarks*, of course, contained a flood of comments on logic and mathematics which are of interest to those concerns, but increasingly it has less to say about philosophy itself. Ostensive definition concerns him again. He has commented on Augustine's use of ostensive definition and says: "One must understand a great deal of a language in order to understand the definition" (p. 9). This is exactly Augustine's conclusion, although Augustine extends it to include knowledge of the object outside language.

Then he comes closer to Kierkegaard: "Is the meaning really only the use of the word?", which he has sometimes indicated. "Isn't it the way this use meshes with our life?" (p. 9). And rather than the understanding of a word dissolving our philosophical puzzles, he states: ""Understanding a word"—that is infinitely various" (p. 11). And grammar takes on a "metaphysical" rather than "logical" meaning: "What belongs to grammar are all the conditions necessary for comparing the proposition with reality —all the conditions necessary for its sense" (p. 13). That is, its meaning comes from the reality to which it refers, not simply from the proposition. Grammar is just an aid. "The connection between "language and reality" is made by definitions of words—which belongs to grammar" (p. 13). But language does not stand independent of reality.

"The task of philosophy is not to create an ideal language, but to clarify the use of existing language" (p. 19). The subtlety is that, if logic and its procedures are your measure, are you not using an artificial product to apply to a naturally fallible phenomenon? He does say: "The philosophy of logic speaks of sentences and words in the sense in which we speak of them in ordinary life" (p. 19). However the operations of logic are not the "ordinary" operations of the mind but are instead something only a few engage in, an esoteric enterprise. Again: "A proposition seems to demand that reality be compared with it" (p. 21). This makes the philosopher's main job to understand "reality," since this

---

[9] eds. Rush Rhees, trans. Anthony Kenney, University of California Press, Berkeley, 1974.

is what propositions must be compared with. And "language" cannot be the same as "reality." If a proposition is a "picture," (p. 25) the comparison still needs to be made, since all the pictures/propositions we have do not say the same thing.

Although Wittgenstein says "It is for philosophy to show that there are no problems," (p. 47) this cannot be true in any literal sense. Otherwise, his own "philosophy" would have no problems if understood properly, which has not been true. Reality does worry Wittgenstein as well as language games. "The connection between 'language and reality' is made by definition of words, and these belong to grammar, so that language remains self-contained and autonomous" (p. 97). But if it is to be "connected" to reality, language cannot remain autonomous else it cannot be compared to reality since the rules, the "grammar," of reality could be quite different from that of language (or logic or mathematics).

If philosophy is to clarify our use of language so as to remove particular misunderstandings (p. 115), it may do this (as Plato did in exploring the definitions of controversial terms). But we cannot be sure that this will clarify reality or remove our misunderstandings. It might, it could, but removing the misunderstandings of language does not in itself guarantee that. Plato is convinced we cannot force another person to learn, although we can correct their grammar. The key to this puzzle may be Wittgenstein's assumed "harmony." "Like everything metaphysical the harmony between thought and reality is to be found in the grammar of language" (p. 162). If examined, that is an odd thought, since the only thing the grammar of language in itself can guarantee is that it applies to language. Language in itself cannot guarantee its "harmony" with reality.

Again he reverts to independence: "Grammar is not accountable to any reality" (p. 184). But if it is self-contained, surely it cannot guarantee its harmony with reality, or that it does or can provide an accurate picture. "Grammar consists of conventions," (p. 190) but if these are of our invention and within our control, for example as symbolic logic has evolved, we cannot at all be sure that the structure of reality reflects our conventions. "No calculus can decide a philosophical problem," (p. 296) he says. This would seem to separate logic, language, and mathematics from "reality." Yet Wittgenstein never does give up the notion that language can lead us to reality. It may, of course, but to lead is not the same as to capture.

It could only occur to a logician to call language a "game," since mathematical logic has all the properties of a game, all the while there is a residual oddness about talking of language as a game. The comparison can be made, of course, and we do say that people play games with us in using words. However, it is not obvious to think of language in this way, and so it will always have a sense of artificial contrivance. Problem: if we do not or cannot think of language as a game, or games, can philosophy then help with the solution of problems, since the premise always remains in question? Of course, many have followed Wittgenstein in talking of language games, but this can be no more than a "fashion" if other approaches to philosophy remain. And is there any way that all can be forced to one philosophical outlook?

In the *Remarks on the Foundations of Mathematics*[10] Wittgenstein did compare logic and thought (but not logic and reality). "The propositions of logic are 'laws of thought,' because they bring out the essence of human thinking," (p. 41e) the technique. "They show what thinking is and also show kinds of thinking" (p. 41e). Unfortunately, the relation between thinking and reality is not established. The two cannot of course be the same, since Wittgenstein rejects solipsism. And the rules for, or the clearing up of, logic/thought brings us no guarantee of a greater grasp of reality. That can be assumed, as Wittgenstein does at times, but the failure of philosophy to become a unified science seems to argue against it.

If "the mathematician is an inventor, not a discoverer," (p. 47e) then mathematical logic is an invention of the mind, which can be "reinvented," and it might teach us little or nothing about reality or how to discover its structure. He does tell us that it is possible for "the sickness of philosophical problems...to get cured only through a changed mode of thought and life..." (p. 57e). However, if we note "changed mode of life," one could then change his or her mode of thought and still not "cure" philosophy's sickness, because the mode of life had not changed along with the thought. This fact is at the center of Kierkegaard's work, and it seems increasingly to dominate Wittgenstein's. He became progressively dissatisfied with his mode of life, all the while his mode of thought was becoming accepted.

One could argue that, just as Wittgenstein refused to accept the reduction of mathematics to symbolic logic, so he never managed to

---

[10] eds. G.H. von Wright, R. Rhees, G.E.M. Anscombe; trans. Anscombe, MIT Press, Cambridge, 1967.

reduce the compelling ethical/religious torments of his life to his philosophical view, which should have clarified them for him. Pragmatism reappears in his remarks, because mathematics does not help philosophy in the long run. "The proof of a proposition shows me what I am prepared to stake on its truth" (p. 186e). "Even God cannot determine something mathematical only by mathematics" (p. 186e). So Wittgenstein increasingly finds that all cannot be reduced to one theoretical base and that life as lived is not only unsolved by theoretical analysis alone, but that theory may have to refer outside of itself if resolution is ever to be achieved for the individual.

G. The Importance of the Momentary and the Random

The *Notebooks* and *Zettel* offer a series of random insights; some are illuminating but seldom systematic. However, more than most of his technical work, they show a Wittgenstein closer to his biography, without which his whole project in philosophy cannot be understood. From the beginning he knew what lay outside technical enclosure, and our only mistake would be to assume that he thought it unimportant. His life demonstrates otherwise, as does his attachment to Tolstoy and Kierkegaard and James. His whole battle seems to have been to find a way to express what he thought important. His lifestyle reflects his attempt to embody this in practice. Both his acceptance of the limits of (technical) language, and his struggle to convey what lies outside, testify to this.

"Logic must take care of itself"[11] (p. 2e). This does not seem to confine all thought to logic but instead to confine logic to its sphere. We can't go wrong in logic, he states, but he knows perfectly well how possible it is to go wrong in life. Yet: "Logic is interested only in reality. And thus in sentences ONLY in so far as they are *pictures* of reality" (p. 9e). But what if the structures of logic in themselves prevent it from "picturing" important aspects of reality? And logic may turn in upon itself: "In propositions we... arrange things *experimentally*, as they do *not* have to be in reality" (p. 13e). Thus, logic does not have to picture reality exactly as it is. It may construct its own house. "A statement cannot be concerned with the logic of the world. The logic of the world is prior to all truth and falsehood" (p. 14e).

Wittgenstein recognizes that "The proposition is a model of reality as we imagine it," (p. 20e) so that it may or may not state what we find

---

[11] Ludwig Wittgenstein, *Notebooks, 1914-1916*, eds. G.H. von Wright, G.E.M.Anscombe, trans. Anscombe. Harper and Row, New York, 1969.

to be true in fact. "The proposition is true when what it imagines exists" (p. 16e). But no amount of logical analysis can tell us that, and it is questionable whether an examination of language can either. Wittgenstein does not give up or shun that which cannot be expressed. It haunts him. "At this point I am again trying to express something that cannot be expressed" (p. 31e). The trouble is that "what can be shown cannot be said," (p. 34e) so that he is caught between two worlds, two incongruous forms of expression. Logic, language have advantages, but they miss much that is important. "What is mirrored in language I cannot use language to express" (p. 42e).

Philosophy is not all: "It is one of the chief skills of the philosopher not to occupy himself with questions which do not concern him" (p. 44e). Yet he cannot give up and confine himself to the logical structure of language, although that offers the only possibility of clarity and finality: "The limits of my language stand for the limits of my world" (p. 49e). But that is a cage in which he is locked and what lies outside is *not* unimportant. "The urge toward the mystical comes of the non-satisfaction of our wishes by science" (p. 51e) or, Wittgenstein might have added, from his inability to confine all that is important to him to either logic or even to philosophy, as he had understood it. Facts are easy, confineable. But "suppose there is something outside the *facts*?" (p. 51e).

"What cannot be expressed we do not express—and how try to *ask* whether THAT can be expressed which cannot be EXPRESSED?" (p. 52e). One can almost say that the "contradiction" expressed here dominated Wittgenstein's work and life. He states: "The great problem round which everything I write turns is: is there an order in the world *a priori*, and if so what does it consist in?" (p. 53e). Wittgenstein answers this by establishing a pristine order for the worlds of logic and mathematics, but he recognizes that these are humanly constructed. In that sense they are "arbitrary" and so not *a priori* as an order for the world we experience. He tried to make language conform to logic but found too much that was important to be still "outside."

"If a proposition tells us something, then it must be a picture of reality just as it is, and a complete picture at that" (p. 61e). Perhaps the problem is that this "reality" turned out to be the constructed reality of the logic of the *Tractatus* and too much of what was important escaped its confines. Language may come to reflect the "really real" but, in its symbolization, its picturing, its limitless variety of forms, it shows its own inability to express all that is. If "the world has a fixed structure,"

(p. 62e) then there is another "world" outside. Vagueness must be accepted, not eliminated artificially. "I only want to justify the vagueness of ordinary sentences, for it *can* be justified" (p. 70e). "What do I know about God and the purpose of life? I know that this world exists" (p. 72e).

But Wittgenstein never suggests that our interest is limited to "this world's" existence. On the contrary, "The meaning of life, i.e., the meaning of the world, we can call God" (p. 73e). "To pray is to think about the meaning of life" (p. 73e). The facts of the world are not the end of the matter. "To believe in God means to see that life has a meaning" (p. 74e). Wittgenstein stated that he could not believe in God, but he always struggled with the question of the meaning of life. This is why his lifestyle was a constant problem, which is the same as to struggle with God, and this requires intensity not belief. "What we are dependent on we can call God" (p. 74e). And Wittgenstein did depend on God, in the sense that he never gave up the struggle for the meaning of life.

Happiness and its quest dogged his tracks. Like Kierkegaard, he recognized that the struggle one needs to engage in to solve the problem is the opposite of happiness: "Only a man who lives not in time but in the present is happy" (p. 74e). This is Kierkegaard's "aesthetic man" who attempts to live only in the present moment, and it may explain Wittgenstein's love of American pulp novels and his absorption with light American movies and musicals. He allows himself to be totally immersed in them, in the present. However, such happiness, being absorbed in the moment, cannot be long lasting. For "conscience is the voice of God," (p. 75e) and the unrelenting struggle with conscience reflected in his biography shows a man heavily burdened by God (in that sense). What lies beyond language is mysterious. But there is more that is closer to home. "The I, the I is what is deeply mysterious" (p. 81e).

Wittgenstein never believed in God as the world's creator, but he did believe that "aesthetically, the miracle is that the world exists" (p. 86e). As Heidegger would put it: why is there something rather than nothing at all? And as one who admittedly thought of suicide, Wittgenstein echoes Camus: "If suicide is allowed, then everything is allowed" (p. 91e). Suicide is the elementary sin, but he does not (or cannot) follow the Existentialists in giving meaning to his life by willing to act and so to define himself. For if philosophical puzzles are the puzzles of language and are "irrelevant to our everyday life,"[12] (p. 1) then philosophy must have something "wrong" in its make up, and those who follow it will be frustrated in so far as they take the problems of everyday life seriously and attend to them.

Consider this quotation and see if it does not seem that Wittgenstein is himself the fly caught in the fly bottle, one who can release others but not himself, because he demands that philosophy do more for him all the while restricting it rigidly. "What distinguishes language from a game in this sense is its application to reality. This application is not shown in grammar, the application of the signs is outside the signs, the picture does not contain its own application. Language is connected with reality by picturing it, but that connection cannot be made in language, explained by language" (p. 10). Thus, there is no way in the world that an analysis of language, whatever clarity it may provide, can of itself provide the connection to reality which we seek.

Philosophy is being reduced to a matter of skill, but what we want is a final answer, some description of the world, whether verifiable or not (p. 21). Wittgenstein reports that we leave aside our initial question about philosophy and "follow the instinct to clarify" (p. 22). But if we do not, can not, get rid of our sense of the urgency of philosophy, then our clarifying activity may be successful, but it will at the same time frustrate the primal "philosopher's urge." If we are "not laying foundations but tidying up a room," (p. 24) that is all right as long as we find that satisfying. Like Kant, he knows that the limits he has set on reason will always make us curious about what lies outside reason's limits. Again like Kant, Wittgenstein gets "to the boundary of language which stops us from asking further questions" (p. 34).

"The fascination of philosophy lies in paradox and mystery," (p. 63) Wittgenstein says. And yet we know that he rejects the notion of paradox in logic and admits mystery in philosophy but puts it outside of what can be spoken. Thus, the fascination of philosophy remains present but is frustrated by the exclusions required by logic and language. What then happens to philosophical fascination if it does not fade away, as it did not do so for Wittgenstein himself? "We cannot talk about the limits of experience, because we should have to experience both sides of the limit," (p. 86) he says again reflecting Kant. Wittgenstein sets limits on

---

[12] *Wittgenstein's Lectures, Cambridge 1930-32*, ed. Desmond Lee, University of Chicago Press, Chicago, 1980.

experience by his constructions in logic and in language, but obviously he continued to experience both sides of these limits.

"Philosophical trouble arises through seeing a system of rules and seeing that things do not fit it"[13] (p. 3). Thus philosophical problems are not solved by experience. But if Wittgenstein qua logician has begun by constructing a system of rules (the *Tractatus*) and then finds that his own experience does not fit within it, how are questions about experience to be answered? Questions of language may "go away" by the analysis of language, but that cannot be the same as saying that the problems of experience, e.g., ethics, religion, will disappear upon the analysis of language. That would be to apply language analysis beyond the limits for which it was designed. Experience is another thing.

As has been noted many times, the further Wittgenstein gets from logic and language, the more he stops saying "true" and "false" and the more he begins to talk of "practical" or "impractical" (e.g., p. 16). He recognizes the affinity between his pointing at mistakes in language and Plato's dialogue method (pp. 27-28), but he believes his is a new activity and can do much that the old method could not do. The questions of meaning are the central questions of philosophy. Is the meaning of a word the list of rules of its use? No. "Plato's talk of looking for the essence of things was very like talk of looking for the *ingredients* in a mixture" (p. 34). "We can only ascertain the meaning of the word "beauty" by seeing how we use it" (p. 36). This of course is the same exercise that is set out in Plato's Dialogues.

"One difficulty with philosophy is that we lack a synoptic view," Wittgenstein tells us (p. 43). We have no map of the country. But "the country we are talking about is language, and the geography is grammar" (p. 43). However, our problem (and Wittgenstein's) is whether this gives us the synoptic view we/he need, or if it only restricts us to some part, i.e., language and grammar. Wittgenstein like others is torn between limiting philosophy's meaning to a highly restricted, artificial structure which we can hope to control and still becoming desperately interested in all that lies beyond these restrictions. "We are constantly mislead," Wittgenstein tells us, "by having the same forms of expression for mathematical and empirical facts" (p. 184).

---

[13] *Wittgenstein's Lectures, Cambridge, 1932-35*, ed. Alice Ambrose, The University of Chicago Press, Chicago, 1982.

The *Zettel*[14] or fragments begin in early 1929, but most are late, 1945-48. In an optimistic note he remarks: "Like every thing metaphysical the harmony between thought and reality is to be found in the grammar of the language" (p. 12e). How convenient that would be, if true. Then, by studying grammar we would discover not something about language and logic, but about thought and reality. However, we know that thought is not always confined to the logical, and what we often discover is a lack or harmony between ourselves and reality. If so, grammar might tell us something about the harmonies internal to language structure but then reach discord where thought and reality were concerned.

"How words are understood is not told by words alone" (p. 26e). That is the problem and one reason why language remains inadequate to the task. The difficulty is that, with life's problems, we don't "understand" by using rules and definitions concerning language and grammar, as we do in logic. Wittgenstein treats language as if it were like logic, but at other times of insight he is painfully aware that language is not used as a "game" if it is not conceived of on the model of logic and, what is more, that our concern with what lies outside the limits of our language (which contains a great deal of philosophy's traditional concerns and which are his concerns also) is perhaps more important to us as individuals.

He tells us: "Compare: inventing a game—inventing a language—inventing a machine" (p. 60e). Yet he also tells us that: "the concept of a living being has the same indeterminacy as that of a language" (p. 60e). But here he uses language in two senses: the invented game vs. the repository of living indeterminacy. Some might say that it was Wittgenstein's aim (or claim) to have invented a method for philosophy to rid ordinary language of its indeterminacy. But if so, we have to ask carefully: is this "language" as it relates itself to reality and to the indeterminacy of living being, or is it "language" as it can be made to reflect the constructed rules of logic and the stipulated definitions of mathematics?

Wittgenstein asks himself: "How does it come about that philosophy is so complicated a structure? It surely ought to be completely simple, if it is the ultimate thing, independent of all experience, that you make it out to be" (p. 81e). So he experiences a paradox, a situation which

---

[14] Edited by G.E.M. Anscombe, G.H. von Wright; trans. G.E.M. Anscombe, University of California Press, Berkeley, 1970.

Kierkegaard found to be edifying. He can make philosophy simple; it can be "ultimate" if it is independent of experience. But then it is an internalized game and does not necessarily clarify or simplify experience, since it has been made independent in order to achieve clarity and rigor. You cannot have it both ways: simple *and* dependent on experience. The fly is caught in the fly bottle of its own construction. Self-imposed limits and rules exclude him from what is of greatest personal, vs. technical, interest.

"Metaphysics obliterates the distinction between factual and conceptual investigations" (p. 82e). True, because it tries to form concepts to capture facts about reality, which the best know they cannot do even while they try, e.g., the mystics whom Wittgenstein emulates. "Only God sees the most secret thoughts," (p. 98e) he remarks, a concept which may have attracted him to Augustine's *Confessions*. But Wittgenstein cannot *believe* in God (vs. his constant *struggle* with God), and so he is barred from exploring his "secret thoughts" as a legitimate source of philosophy. They are out of bounds to technical schemes, known only to a God whom he cannot believe in. His motto is: "Let us not be bewitched" (p. 119e). Inside language games, certainly not; outside language games, he knows he cannot help but be.

The *Zettel* ends with Wittgenstein saying: "You can't hear God speak to someone else, you hear him only if you are being addressed," (p. 124e) just as Martin Buber tells us in *I and Thou*. But then he adds: that is a grammatical remark. Now, if that is what grammar teaches, then we see "grammar" in a whole new light. Surely the address of God is heard by no one else, as he indicates, which would make it a "private language" such as he ruled impossible. And if God is not within ordinary language but involves an extraordinary hearing, that defines the limits of language and the rules of grammar. Wittgenstein must have known of, and approved, the famous Old Testament phrase: "My ways are not your ways."

Given the obvious mounting tension in Wittgenstein's life, and the parallel tension in his professional life (his ambivalence toward students, teaching and publishing; his dissatisfaction with his personal relationships and his geographical location), why does he not burst the boundaries of both the *Tractatus* and the *Investigations* and write on religion and reality and life? His whole professional life has committed him to the limitations of philosophy as he defined it, even by the changes in his theory that he makes. As Kant says, that which is not derived from experience but is *a priori* cannot overstep its bounds and apply itself to that outside the source of its derivation (to the world in itself). Wittgenstein must suffer depression: the philosophy he has constructed cannot be applied beyond its limits, because its strength is derived from its limitation.

H. COLOR, AND PSYCHOLOGY, AND STATES OF MIND

Surely the not inconsiderable later writings of Wittgenstein on these specified topics, which have narrowed many philosophers down to what they call philosophy of mind, must strike one as amazingly at odds with Wittgenstein's lifestyle as it escalates. And so it is. Our theme is that while life thrusts immense and traditional ethical/religious questions on him (largely without hope of personal resolution), his whole fantastic effort of philosophical construction (something of a tour de force) restricts him from turning his professional skills to the area of his greatest growing personal concern. He reportedly called Kierkegaard "one of the great philosophers." And it is not too much to suggest that this is because Kierkegaard's published works were an embarrassing reflection of his personal struggle.

Although these are *Remarks On Color*,[15] Wittgenstein comments early on: "In every serious philosophical question uncertainty extends to the very roots of the problem" (p. 4e, 15). There could hardly be a greater contrast to the *Tractatus* claim of finality or even to the *Investigations* claim of a method to produce clarity and banish perplexity. He wants to establish a "logic of color concepts" (p. 5e, 22). But given the whole effort to date, it is hard to see why it would end here. It is easy to see that "states of mind" offer endless possibilities for analysis, but Wittgenstein could not have thought these would settle much.

"In philosophy we must always ask, 'How must we look at this problem in order for it to become solvable'" (p. 15e,11). It is clear that ethical/religious problems are not, by their nature, "solvable," so Wittgenstein turns to psychology instead. But he finds little there of what concerns him, except technically. Is that why he complains in later years of how dry he is in philosophy. True, earlier he had remarked that philosophers were only creative for a short period of time in their youth (something said of mathematicians also). But Wittgenstein's own most important philosophical innovations were made later and without those little interest would have been sustained in the *Tractatus*. Thus, we

---

[15] ed. G.E.M. Anscombe, trans. McAlister & Schätte, University of California Press, Berkeley, 1978.

might have expected an expansion of philosophy in his mature years, not its narrow restriction.

One remark interjected into the discussion of color may be helpful: "Here I would like to make a general observation concerning the nature of philosophical problems. Lack of clarity is tormenting. It is felt shamefully. We feel: we do not know our way about where we *should* know our way about. And nevertheless it *isn't* so. We can get along very well without these distinctions *and* without knowing our way about here" (p. 21e, 33). This is a startlingly candid remark and somewhat of a jolt for anyone who has worked his or her way through the *Tractatus* or *Investigations*, etc., which stress clarifying and eliminating puzzles. It is not a tired remark, but it is one which could lift a lot of restrictions from philosophy which was sometimes narrowed considerably.

Following Wittgenstein in philosophy, as he tells us, "one must always be prepared to learn something totally new" (p. 23e, 45). But he feared his students would simply become disciples and wish to hang onto and defend what they thought they had understood, rather than move constantly forward. The history of Wittgenstein interpretation largely confirms his fears, a dilemma which haunted Kierkegaard too. Could the following remark come from one of the strict Wittgenstein "clarifiers"? "When someone who believes in God looks around him and asks: 'Where did everything I see come from?' ...he is *not* asking for a (causal) explanation... He is expressing an attitude toward all explanation,—but how is this shown in his life?" (p. 58e, 317). God need not have a large part in one's intellectual life, but God may demand a "showing" in our ascetic practice.

"God" is shut out of clear expression in language, as is the mystical, by the restriction on meaningful discourse which Wittgenstein imposed. But he is not the first to suggest this. Every major theologian, and every mystic, has struggled with the inadequacy, perhaps the impossibility, of adequate expression where God is concerned. True, the Modern world, beginning with Descartes, thought God to be the epitome of a "clear and distinct idea." But they were obsessed with the finality of their methodology, whereas Wittgenstein from the beginning was of two minds about the ability of any language to express all we need to consider. Our concerns are always wider than our language competency.

In addition to color Wittgenstein's *Last Writings*[16] indicate his increasing interest in "describing mental states" (pp. I-6e, 30). This is an introversion that created "philosophy of mind," and it stands in glaring contrast to the increasing tension in Wittgenstein's life and in his relationship to philosophy. He does remark: "In philosophy one must distinguish between propositions that express our mental inclination, and those that *solve* problems" (p. I-17e, 109). Philosophy of mind is clearly about mental inclinations and thus makes no claim to *solve* problems. But this does not mean they do not need solving. Rilke has told us that we must not seek answers but instead learn to love the questions. Wittgenstein, who early on had "answers," speaks reflexively in this late work: "It's no accident that I'm using so many interrogative sentences in this book" (p. I- 22e, 150).

Kierkegaard was fascinated with the future as compared to Hegel's absorption in the historical. Wittgenstein agrees that the future is opaque: "Nothing is so well hidden as future events. They *can't* be known. One can only know what is happening now" (p. I-27e, 186). Presumably the analysis of language would not help us here, since the propositions have not been formed. "Human nature determines what is capricious" (p. I-46e, 329). He who sought and defined clarity says: "The greatest difficulty in these investigations is to find a way of representing vagueness" (p. I-48e, 347). Note that he does not say to eradicate all unclarity but rather to represent it.

Our problem with God has always been to attempt to represent vagueness. Yet that is not all that defies expression. "I can recognize a genuine loving look, distinguish it from a pretended one. And yet there is no way in which I can describe it to someone else" (p. I-122, 937). The demand for clarity and precision in language excludes both loving looks and God and yet these are of real concern. The limits language places on philosophical expression are becoming more problematical. Volume One ends with the soul: "The idea of the human soul... is very similar to the idea of the meaning of a word, which stands next to the word" (p. I-127e, 979). Words we know and see; meaning is not quite such an obvious process. Perhaps its similarity to the notion of soul attracts Wittgenstein to "meaning."

If, as Wittgenstein says, "there is uncertainty of behavior which doesn't stem from uncertainty of thought," (p. II-113e, 660) clarifying

---

[16] *On the Philosophy of Psychology*, 3 vols., ed. von Wright and Nyman, trans. Luckhardt & Aue, University of Chicago Press, Chicago, 1982.

language may have little effect upon behavior. Unclarities, once cleared up in philosophy, may then be of little practical use to us, and Wittgenstein has said that we determine meaning by use. In this case the meaning will stay vague as long as our behavior remains vague, since that is the source of meaning. "For words have meaning only in the stream of life" (p. II-116e, 687). But is the "stream of life" the same as intellectual language games? I suggest that Wittgenstein tends increasingly to think not.

Wittgenstein has opposed the idea of contradiction in logic. Yet in his increasingly Pragmatic approach, he shifts. ""This is beautiful and this is not beautiful" is a contradiction, but it has a use" (p. III-9e, 37). "But aren't you a pragmatist?" he asks himself, and he replies: "No. For I am not saying that a proposition is true if it is useful" (p. III-54e, 266). This does distinguish Wittgenstein from James who did say that the proposition "becomes true." But this is not the same as saying that truth in a logical-linguistic sense is useful. That is a matter of experiment and individual assessment, and it may also be more important. If "the human being is the best picture of the human soul," (p. III-56e, 281) we know that the concept "soul" has a basis in experience.

"The way you use the word "God" shows, not whom you mean, but what you mean" (p. III-91e, 475). "God," then, is not Descartes' clear and distinct idea but might be closer to Spinoza's elaborate exploration of "Substance." Yet in spite of turning considerable attention to psychology and the elucidation of mental states, Wittgenstein is not optimistic about the resolution of the problems encountered: "...in psychology one is completely uncertain of the fruitfulness of the experiments" (p. III-180e, 1039). There is what is problematic and there are experiments, "but they quite bypass the thing that is worrying us" (p. III-180e, 1039). This late comment on the Philosophy of Psychology could just as well stand for Wittgenstein's appraisal of his philosophical method and its application to his life's concerns.

3 Wittgenstein and Some of His Interpreters

A. Finality and Non-Finality in Philosophy

It is clear that the *Tractatus* sought finality in philosophy, but it is even more clear that Wittgenstein rejected this goal in his later work. The *Investigations* still has "Modernist" overtones in the sense that finality of theory is not sought but a certain finality of method is advocated. However, unlike Descartes clear and distinct ideas or Spinoza's method for improving the understanding or Locke's empiricism, Wittgenstein began in the *Tractatus* by limiting philosophy. And yet like Kant, he recognized the enduring importance and fascination of that which lies outside the domain of clear expression. What the *Investigations* adds is a non-systematic element which makes final interpretation an impossibility.

One could argue that it is not possible to understand Wittgenstein without understanding Kierkegaard, whom he admired. The *Tractatus* began with Wittgenstein's fascination, and then disagreement, with Russell and Frege over logic and mathematics. He early on read Schopenhauer and had grown to like James' *Varieties of Religious Experience*, plus his encounter with Tolstoy (to be examined later). Kierkegaard fought Hegel's systematization, and Wittgenstein's later writings have an intentional non-systematic mold. No final dialectic can be traced leading to a synthesis, so that a "dogmatic" treatment of Wittgenstein is the only one we know that must be rejected.

Kierkegaard told us that no one would be able to find a single key which would render all his writing consistent. However, like Wittgenstein, he actually does give us an overview of his work, after claiming that such is impossible. Innovators cannot help but feel the power of their discoveries, even when the core of the discovery is the impossibility of finality in theory. However, more important in our comparison of this "odd couple" in philosophy is Kierkegaard's limitation on reason vs. Wittgenstein's limits on language. Kierkegaard has said that the chief task of the understanding is to understand that there are things it cannot understand. Wittgenstein is equally sure of the importance of matters which lie beyond our language's powers of expression.

Wittgenstein must have known of the early Jewish prohibition on uttering the name of God and the story that anyone who touched the Ark could be struck dead. What exceeds our rational capacities is not unimportant. Rather, we must begin by recognizing the limits in our approach. Although the *Tractatus* seeks a tighter system of philosophy, it ends being very aware of what lies outside its domain. Only the Rationalists (Kierkegaard's enemy, too) cannot understand that what is beyond reason's grasp may be dealt with, just not in discursive forms. The later Wittgenstein is more pluralistic in approach, and in his growing pragmatism he allows what exceeds clear formulation to be dealt with by measuring its effect in our action.

Max Black confines his analysis to the *Tractatus*, which does need commentary.[1] He comments on the meaning of difficult or obscure expressions, and then he finds that there are cryptical or puzzling passages. This form of "textual analysis" is much needed, but it does not set that text in the wider range of Wittgenstein's writings or against his life. In 1964 it was not really possible to do that. If we confine commentary to technical elucidation, we could miss the wider thrust of Wittgenstein's work. Black cites the theme: "language is the great *mirror* in which the logical network is reflected, 'shown,' manifested" (p. 3). For instance, "Wittgenstein was absorbed by this ancient puzzle of the connection between thought and reality," Black tells us (p. 5). But perhaps Wittgenstein took "reality" to be only what emerges in the whole of his life and work.

Our intention is not to do a review of commentaries on Wittgenstein. That would be an enormous undertaking; rather it is simply to set a few against the context of his life. And Black agrees that Wittgenstein sought in logic answers to questions in a self-contained system and that he thought ordinary language could be "in perfect logical order" (p. 6). But then the relation of language to "reality" becomes the chief question. Black remarks that all that was important to

---

[1] *A Companion to Wittgenstein's Tractatus*, Cornell University Press, Ithaca, New York, 1964.

Wittgenstein, aesthetics, ethics, religion, he located in a "transcendental heaven" (p. 10). But could it be these vital interests which tear apart the beautiful symmetry sought in the *Tractatus*?

If Wittgenstein early on sees a necessary connection between language and the world "which guarantees that if one makes sense it will be sense *about the world*," (p. 14) then if he becomes increasingly concerned with the importance of what language cannot (is forbidden to) say, the hope of exploring language as a key to reality is broken. Language may not lead us to, or in fact may block us from, what we most need to explore. Wittgenstein was, as Black remarks, "obsessed by the 'trans-empirical'... that held its author in thrall" (p. 18). Then how shall the trans-empirical be approached if language is not a trustworthy vehicle? Language may be "a 'mirror' of the world," (p. 27) but that "world" proves not to be either all of reality or all that concerns us.

"He locates value outside the world" (p. 373). There is a "mystical" feeling that the world is limited, "that there is something beyond the world" (p. 373). "To the realm of the mystical belongs everything that Wittgenstein regards as having authentic value" (p. 373-74). His urge toward the mystical, Black concludes, "is one of the chief motive powers of the book" (p. 374). Yet the *Tractatus* blocks him from elaborating and exploring it. No wonder that he repudiated much of what he argued to be true in that early book, and this may also account for the "strange" mode of writing and teaching which began to emerge. His amazing technical skill still comments endlessly on logic and mathematics, but his limited "philosophy" blocks him from progress on the levels most important to him.

Black comments on the cryptic passage at the end, "He must throw away the ladder, after he has ascended it," and Black rightly sees this as similar to the skeptical claim of Sextus Empiricus (p. 377). However, the skeptic and the mystic are very close together in basic approach, as Hume noted too. Black does not elaborate on the mystical tradition, which is what clearly is close to Wittgenstein. As the approach to God is near, Bonaventure in *The Mind's Road to God* quotes scripture: "Man shall not see me and live." And he replies: "Let us go forth into darkness and die." The mystic needs to abandon all the intellectual paraphernalia he/she has used in the search. This is classic in the literature.

The conclusion of the *Tractatus*, "What can't be said must be left in silence" (6.54-7) should not be left alone but compared to the long tradition on the edification of silence. It is a necessity for the Trappist or for any monastic life, a path to which Wittgenstein we know was drawn.

Silence is not an abandonment of the quest. It is placing the search, at last, in the right context. After the Holocaust experience, why was Elie Wiesel silent for ten years? And even today he is unwilling to speak either about that or about God, except as story telling and by symbolic indirection. That is a proper feeling of awe any Jew feels in approaching the holy of holies. We have learned much in the *Tractatus*. But in the tradition a "learned ignorance," we have now learned how much we do not know. Socratic Wisdom!

Oddly, after all this Black ends his book with a defense of the classic modern quest for clarity. "For clarity arrives at the end of conceptual investigation, not at its beginning," (p. 386) which completely turns around the important conclusion with which Wittgenstein wanted to leave us. Clarity in logic and mathematics, perhaps even in language, yes. Clarity about "reality" and all that lies beyond language, no, except that we are clear about the limits of language. And it is clear that much of importance lies beyond clear expression. But are we not to speak of it (6.54-7)? Wittgenstein's later work will explore "living it," testing it in practice, not ignoring conceptual problems, but exploring other avenues of approach.

In bringing together a group of essays on Wittgenstein, George Pitcher[2] says that they will not deal with his life and character nor with the *Tractatus*, "that deeply esoteric work" (p. vi). To single out the *Investigations* may be to misunderstand it, if its radical innovations in fact are primarily due to the "esoteric" parts of the *Tractatus*, plus their importance to Wittgenstein as a philosopher and the fact that the *Tractatus* was unsuccessful in its attempts to treat reality with the clarity of logic and language. Quinton comments: Wittgenstein assumed "the posture of the founder of a religion rather than that of the exponent of a philosophy" (p. 3). But what if philosophy proves inadequate to the task?

Yet Quinton in his opening essay tells us, "there is what might be called the deep nonsense, the transcendental or mystical profundities of morality and religion" (p. 8). The problem with this is that "nonsense" must be carefully understood. Morality and religion only become so when philosophers use language to try to make conclusive statements. Descartes notion that "God" is the most clear and distinct idea in our mind is just such "deep nonsense," precisely due to the absurd proposal

---

[2] *Wittgenstein: The Philosophical Investigations*, University of Notre Dame Press, Notre Dame, 1968.

that God can be captured in a clear idea, not because these matters are not of vital concern to philosophers as well as to ordinary folks. The *Tractatus*, Pitcher notes, saw language as a logically rigid essence. In the *Investigations*, language is accepted as living, unsystematic, and polymorphous (p. 9). Why? Coming up against its limits sets rigidity and finality in language in disarray.

Wittgenstein could have gone with the Logical Positivists and attempted to restrict philosophy rigidly, but we know that he rejected that. Yet Quinton admits that two generations of British philosophers (as quoted previously) "have derived from each of his books a coherent and comprehensive philosophical system" (p. 10). This is almost shocking and surely seems to miss a great deal of what was most urgent for Wittgenstein to convey. The so-called "self-denying" comments of Wittgenstein about the limits of philosophy and language do not destroy philosophy. Its precision and any possible finality must be set in the context of a larger enterprise.

B. Completing Wittgenstein

Robert Fogelin's book[3] agrees that Wittgenstein is often obscure and that his texts offer few arguments. For the *Tractatus*, "this interplay between a structure of necessary connections (logical space) and a purely contingent set of items embedded in it (the totality of facts) is fundamental to the Tracterian world view" (p. 4). He then proceeds to an exposition of fundamental concepts in the *Tractatus*, e.g. picturing, proposition, etc. But "the theory of propositional meaning... is self-destructive" (p. 89). Wittgenstein's own remarks lack propositional status. Once we understand the form of a proposition, the theme emerges: the insignificance of the sayable (p. 90).

What are the consequences for philosophy if in fact "it is quite impossible to express the essential character of language or the world in a proposition" (p. 90)? The underlying structure of language emerges, not in the symbolization of everyday language, but in the actual employment of this symbolism. "What signs fail to express, their application shows" (p, 91). Where logical rigor fails, pragmatism emerges. "The *Tractatus* places very narrow limits on what can be said," (p. 92) and the whole of ethics/religion lies outside, but its value and our intensity about it are affirmed not denied. This leads us to ask: "What moves us to initiate philosophical reflection?" (p. 97).

---

[3] *Wittgenstein*, Routledge & Kegan Paul, London, 1976.

Concluding that the standpoint of the *Tractatus* does not work, even on its own terms, Fogelin admits that the *Investigations* "seems to defy sweeping generalizations" (p. 206). Wittgenstein moves away from the assertion that words gain their meaning by standing for things, and moves toward a view that "the philosopher has no business constructing theories or defending theses" (p. 206). This is a movement away from a proxy theory of meaning, as Fogelin summarizes it. "Yet the full articulation of the constructivist theory" remains to be done (p. 207). Wittgenstein's later philosophy is important, but "it is also radically incomplete," Fogelin concludes (p. 207). The problem is that, again, this remark suggests that it *can* be "completed."

In different ways, yet apparently with the same intent, Wittgenstein has like Kierkegaard gone to great lengths to make his views incomplete, and to avoid acting as if they could or should be or that he wanted this done. He was suspicious of the motives of his students and afraid they would make his work easy, when he had fought to make it difficult if not impossible. More important, any "completion" can only be done by focusing on one aspect and ignoring other major themes and concerns. Kierkegaard tried a summary for himself in his *Point of View*, but again he could do this and "contradict" his own warnings against systematizationsystematization only by ignoring some of the most important aspects of his writings. From the *Tractatus* on, Wittgenstein has warned us how much of importance lies outside the net of any language.

C. Ayer and Positivism

A.J. Ayer's book, *Wittgenstein*,[4] offers an interesting chance to consider Wittgenstein's "flirtations" with Positivism and to ask why he so quickly saw that his aims were opposed to the Vienna Circle. Schlick was an admirer of the *Tractatus* and saw in it Wittgenstein's claim to have "supplied the definitive solutions to all the problems of philosophy, so far as they were solvable" (p. 5). This was parallel, if not similar, to the goals of the Vienna Circle. But what was not properly appreciated was how much of importance lay outside the net of language and how interested Wittgenstein was in this. Ayer quotes von Wright: "Wittgenstein received deeper impressions from some writers in the borderland between philosophy, religion and poetry than from

---

[4] University of Chicago Press, Chicago, 1985.

philosophers" (p. 14). If that is true, in spite of his logic-mathematical bent, his aims are other than Positivism.

Ayer quotes Russell's question: "Wittgenstein, are you thinking about logic or your sins? 'Both,' he said, and then reverted to silence" (p. 16). Such is not the mood of the Vienna Circle, and "There is a tension in his thought," Ayer notes (p. 19). When all possible scientific questions have been answered, "the problems of life remained untouched" (p. 19). Wittgenstein opposed philosophy to science rather than reducing philosophy to it. "In philosophy we must do away with explanation and let description take its place" (p. 67). This opens the door rather widely. However, Ayer's chapter on "Magic and Religion" brings out Wittgenstein's widest divergence from Positivism.

In place of moral theory, Ayer tells us, Wittgenstein draws attention to types of experience which he chose to describe in religious terms. We know that he read James' *Varieties of Religious Experience* with approval. Yet Ayer finds Wittgenstein's conception of "important nonsense" to be "mysterious" (p. 87). Religious theory and practice are quite separate. "The breakdown of theory need not keep good people from religious practice" (p. 90). Ayer remarks that he himself would want some assurance that his beliefs were "true," but to say that is to miss the whole of Wittgenstein's point. Like Kierkegaard, he finds religious belief beyond proof and takes that as its demand for commitment. Ayer wishes that Wittgenstein's pronouncement "had been less oracular," (p. 128) but even to say this misses Wittgenstein's amazing blend of logic and mysticism.

Members of the Vienna Circle "had no indulgence at all for mysticism" and saw that "a hankering after the unsayable was latent in the *Tractatus*" (p. 130). Ayer reports that he cannot acquiesce to "the limitation which he [Wittgenstein] sought to impose upon philosophy" (p. 143). But Ayer misses the whole point that religion and ethics cannot be included but nevertheless exert increasing attraction. Wittgenstein had not "grown tired of thinking," (p. 134) as Ayer suspects. He was increasingly torn by all that lay outside technical analysis and over how one should deal with this. As he reported to Russell, Wittgenstein had the monk's strong sense of sin. He had to deal with it, but it did not fit within formal philosophy as he had defined it.

Saul Kripke's book[5] can be considered along with Ayer's, since he treats Wittgenstein in a technical manner, leaving all the rest behind. There is no attempt to deal with the author's work as a whole. His theme: "Wittgenstein's skeptical problem and argument are important, deserving serious consideration" (p. 12). Kripke notes the difficulty of trying to deal with anything of Wittgenstein's in a clear, definite manner, since the *Investigations* has the form of a "perpetual dialectic," not a systematic work. To attempt "to present Wittgenstein's arguments precisely is to some extent to falsify it" (p. 5). Yet like the systematizers of Kierkegaard who ignore his warnings about the impossibility of completion, Kripke moves ahead to do his best, leaving unanswered what the wider implications might be of Wittgenstein's elusiveness.

Anthony Kenny's book, *Wittgenstein*,[6] concentrates on his philosophy of language and mind. Helpful as this may be, it is not set within the larger project of Wittgenstein's concerns. Kenny reports: "Throughout his life Wittgenstein stood outside philosophical schools and despised contemporary fashions of thought" (p. 1). Kenny concludes that Wittgenstein remained hostile to the proofs for the existence of God, and that "the right method of philosophy consists in putting a stop to metaphysics" (p. 229 and p. 231). But to say this gives one a completely distorted view of how Wittgenstein wanted to treat all of importance that lay outside the bounds of proof. He did not dismiss it; far from it.

D. "Wittgenstein's Conception of Philosophy"

K.T. Fann's book by this name[7] does us a service by putting questions concerning any of Wittgenstein's views in the context of what he wanted philosophy to achieve. We will argue shortly that, for important reasons, this must include his biography and the record of his personal struggle. But since Wittgenstein limits "philosophy" so strictly, we sometimes fail to see what his intellectual life struggled with (and it can be labeled as little else) and sought to achieve. How can "philosophy" have a wider connotation, as well as his familiar narrow, technical definition, or more properly, "definitions"? The chief saga is how Wittgenstein changed his mind about what philosophy is and about its usefulness or uselessness in his life-setting.

---

[5] *Wittgenstein on Private Rules and Language*, Harvard University Press, Cambridge, 1982.
[6] Harvard University Press, Cambridge, 1973.
[7] University of California Press, 1971.

Fann tells us that Wittgenstein doesn't attempt to "answer" questions but to question the questions themselves (p. xii). But if Hegel and Descartes, for example, gave us answers, Plato and Kierkegaard only question questions. This is not a new task for philosophy, then, except the added notion that as a result "the philosophical questions should themselves *completely* disappear" (p. xii). This leads us to ask: what happened in Wittgenstein's life when they did not disappear but rather intensified? If philosophical questions arise "from our misunderstanding of the logic of our language," (p. xiii) what happens when what is important lies "beyond language"?

Wittgenstein underlines this crucial dilemma: "My work consists of two parts: the one presented here plus all that I have *not* written. And it is precisely this second part that is the important one," (p. 1) as Fann quotes him. You face a dilemma, if you are a philosopher and not an actor/dancer, if what is important lies outside of what you have written, and if moreover you begin to feel that it cannot be written. Perhaps the "cryptic" style of the early *Tractatus* should have tipped off both Wittgenstein and his readers. What is oracular in tone and cryptic in is implication cannot hope to be clear, and thus it ultimately frustrates finality. One who uses paradox to convey important thoughts dooms the clear trivialities to receive the greater attention from those intent on achieving "understanding."

First of all, British philosophy as Wittgenstein encountered it liked clarity in argument and lucidity in style as primary virtues. Thus, if it had not been for Wittgenstein's genius in logic, would he have received wide attention? He wrote to Russell: "I believe that I have solved our problem finally" (quoted fn. p. 4). But Wittgenstein assumed that the structure of language is revealed by logic: "Logic is ... a mirror of the world" (T.6.13). Yet if one gradually becomes convinced that the structure of language is not identical with logic, logic will never reveal "the world." Then one needs to turn to imprecise human beings to understand both the meaning and the use of language.

If logic does not share a completely common structure with language, "the world" may exceed the grasp of both. Wittgenstein's now famous "picture-theory" of propositions is an attempt to deal with this. The structure of logic, the structure of language, and the structure of the world are not identical. But "language is a mirror-image of the world" (p. 21). However, the puzzling thing is to figure out if the mirror is distorted so that the "pictures" in propositions, in language, might not reveal the world fully. To one only interested in an internal game of logic, this does not matter. When Wittgenstein later treats language on the model of a game, he is expanding the structure of language (and its function) beyond the structural limits of logic. But this only enlarges the puzzle of whether language does, or even can, reflect reality fully.

The propositions of logic and of ethics are attempts to transcend in language the limits of language. Nevertheless, "there are important things [note, not unimportant] (moral and aesthetic values, meaning of life, etc.) that, although they cannot be *said*, can be *shown*" (p. 22). "They are what is mystical" (T.6.522). The delineation of what can be said and what cannot be said but only shown, is "the cardinal problem of philosophy" (p. 22). But if this involves "the mystical" and if this is of importance, then the whole focus of philosophy, which first shifted away from the structure of logic, now begins to shift away from language, as his increasing stress on practice and pragmatism indicates

Philosophical propositions are "attempts to say things which cannot be said." These are not to be cut off, as Positivism suggested but which Wittgenstein rejected. Religion, ethics, art and the realm of the personal are, like metaphysics, concerned with what cannot be said" (p. 23). "The sense of the world must lie outside the world" (T.6.41). That does not matter if one does not care about those things. But Wittgenstein was vitally concerned, and the clear net of logic had not captured them for him. Language itself began to move further away, in his mind, from logic, although he continued until the end to deal in logic and mathematical problems. It is just that his intellectual and private life faced schizophrenia.

If "God does not reveal himself in the world," (T.6.43) it is not the case that one can say that God does not exist (Wittgenstein is clear about that impossibility) and it certainly does not mean that God is unimportant. If one is not interested, the "mystical" world can be ignored, since it is outside language. But if one's life is involved, one cannot use philosophy to deal with the matter directly. "There are, indeed, things that are inexpressible. They *show* themselves. They are what is mystical" (T.6.522). Many of Wittgenstein's interpreters and clarifiers have been uninterested in the difficult realm of Wittgenstein's life. But his later work gives us every indication that his interest in what lay outside language only increased.

If "the sense of the world must lie outside the world," (T.6.41) if "God does not reveal himself *in* the world," (T.6.432) if there are things that are inexpressible that *show* themselves, "they are what is mystical" (T.6.522). The philosopher, in this case Wittgenstein, is indeed in a strange situation. All that explains, all of personal value, lies outside the limits that have been placed on what can be spoken. The philosopher is in the fly bottle and all that he/she longs for is locked outside, showing itself but out of contact. The inexpressible is precisely all that is important in life. One does not gain sustenance from logic; one plays games with it.

We have a tendency to thrust against the limits of language, that is, as Wittgenstein has erected the barrier, of course. And he is not a Positivist. "But what men mean when they say 'The world exists' lies close to my heart" (p. 28, fn. 3). For propositions to be "nonsensical" does not mean that they are without value or interest but simply that they do not fall within the rigidly established grammatical, logical rules. However, the inexpressible can be shown by music, art, religion. The-later-Wittgenstein will expand on these and break the rigid hold the *Tractatus* placed on language, thus also severing its formal ties to technical logic, which is left to its own world.

When Wittgenstein states: "The solution of the problem of life is seen in the vanishing of the problem," (T.6.521) we might see this as parallel to the "illumination" which the Zen novice seeks. The problem is not disregarded, not unimportant, but it must not to be approached with logic and language head on. As we know, the earlier unsolvable contradictions Wittgenstein encountered in the *a priori* method of the *Tractatus* led him to investigate the actual use of language, which proves to be much broader, less precise, and not structured in exactly the manner of a logical system. As we also know, he went to teach elementary school children (a traumatic experience). Perhaps it is there that he saw the varieties of actual language use.

As Kierkegaard claimed to have restored psychology as "the queen of the sciences," Wittgenstein shifts in the *Investigations* to epistemological and psychological concepts. Following this route he shifts toward a "pragmatic" approach, borrowing from William James. The concept that language always functions in one way is broken, or at least the attempt to fit all actual usage into one logically tight structure is abandoned. The search for "one essence" is dismissed, as James recommended. Language is not the only way to "show" the world, but only one form of symbolism. And since so much of importance lies beyond the grasp of language, life-employment and our use become important.

The early Wittgenstein wrote monologues; the later Wittgenstein is more Socratic in his writing and in his teaching. His early pronouncements were like "divine revelations." For the later Wittgenstein, discussion is essential for learning. The *Tractatus* believed that there must be a final analysis of language connected to the picture theory. It is odd that, when this is rejected and philosophy is opened in its conception, so many take Wittgenstein to be narrowing it to "language analysis." We know that, from early to late, what is most important cannot be confined there. Certainly, one gets a broad spectrum of clues by examining how language is learned and how it is employed. Technical philosophy is circumscribed in its limits, but not the interests of the philosopher. Positivism is rejected.

In actual language "many propositions are vague, inexact, and indefinite but serve our purposes perfectly well" (p. 58). "Inexact" does not mean "unusable." Whereas it was once assumed that the process of analysis could make the sense of propositions clear and explicit, the notion of analysis is now itself under severe criticism. Analysis is no longer the main philosophical method for Wittgenstein. An aspect of the matter can be lost in the "analyzed" form. He ridicules the analyst as someone who "tried to find the real artichoke by stripping it of its leaves" (*Philosophical Investigations*, §164). Language analysis can distort reality.

No wonder Wittgenstein feared what his interpreters would do, as Kierkegaard did. When one is "unusual" in his thought, as both were, misunderstandings are the order of the day. "Use" takes precedence over "meaning" for Wittgenstein. "Don't ask for meaning, ask for use" (p. 68, quoting from John Wisdom). Social as well as linguistic contexts are needed to understand use. The demand for a general theory of meaning of words is useless (p. 69, quoting from G. E. Moore). In shifting to the instrumentality or pragmatic concept of language, Wittgenstein tells us: it is interesting to compare the multiplicity of tools in language and the ways they are used... with what logicians have said about the structure of language (p. 70). And this includes the author of the *Tractatus*.

Language is not the first subject matter of philosophy, but troubles in our thoughts can result in errors, which leads him to discuss language. All philosophy does not dissolve if analysis eliminates errors, only that which stands in the way of our dealing with the world. Linguistic function is more important than linguistic form. The eternal striving for exactness and precision is illusion; vagueness is accepted as reality, in so far as it serves ordinary purposes (p. 82). Philosophy is "a battle against the bewitchment of our intelligence by means of language" (*Investigations*, as quoted p. 87). "Philosophy leaves everything as it is" (*Investigations*, as quoted p. 88).

"Nonsense" is produced in trying to express by the use of language what ought to be embodied in grammar. Or in the *Tractatus*, "nonsense" is produced by attempting to say what cannot be said. But lest this is thought to be a rejection of all but logic, language, and grammar, we need to remember that which is beyond language was never said to be unimportant. "He criticizes metaphysics because it has been presented in empirical form, not because it deals with unimportant matters" (p. 94). Taken at their face value, metaphysical statements are absurd because they appear to make the unexpressible clear, but the "idea expressed in them is of enormous importance" (p. 95).

If as he says the greatest metaphysical writings of the past are among the noblest productions of the human mind, we miss "the whole driving force of the *Investigations* if it is not seen continually to point beyond itself" (p. 96). Remember that Wittgenstein often expresses his most important insights in analogies, metaphors, and parables. If so, in what sense would it make sense to call Wittgenstein an "ordinary language" philosopher? The confusion comes because he increasingly points to ordinary language for insight to help us with puzzles in more sophisticated language. However in no sense could this be because he thought all of importance was in ordinary language. He is on record as saying that this can't be so.

Fann points out that it is important to remember that, by design, there is no "system" in Wittgenstein's later philosophy (p. 101), which makes all final statements about his views an impossibility. If the goal of philosophy is to make philosophical problems disappear, this can only refer to all that lies within language, not all that lies beyond, which we are left to deal with in other ways. Nowhere could it possibly be shown that he thought all human concerns lie within language. They admittedly do not. To write or talk Ethics or Religion is "to run against the boundaries of language" (p.104). "Wittgenstein was a passionate thinker for whom philosophical problems appeared as tormenting "personal" problems" (p. 105). One might say that he wished every human problem did lay within the reach of language.

It makes sense to suggest that he found Augustine's *Confessions* his natural form of expression, since Augustine, Kierkegaard and Dostoyevsky were his favorite philosophers. He agreed that a philosophical treatise might contain nothing but questions (without answers) (p. 109, quoting from Malcolm). But like the Buddha and the

Zen master, Wittgenstein is concerned to give peace to those who are tormented by abstract philosophical questions. That is far from saying that the problems are not real. The opposite must be true. However, all these masters agree that the novice may have approached the problems in a wrong way. The strictness of the master, plus rigorous ascetic practice, alone can cure that and explain the secret properly.

4 WITTGENSTEIN AND HIS BIOGRAPHERS

A. How Biography Illuminates Language

If Wittgenstein has made us all think more about language, its help and its harm, than we did before his writing became public, there is reason to think that his biography may illuminate his views about language use. Ray Monk's authoritative work is our main concern and is the occasion for re-evaluating Wittgenstein's intent, but two short works by colleagues who knew him well personally offer an initial contrast. G.E.M. Anscombe, one of Wittgenstein's trusted literary executors, gives us *An Introduction to Wittgenstein's Tractatus*.[1] It is of course helpful. But like many interpretations, it offers mainly a clarification of concepts.

In his Foreword, H.J. Paton tells us that Wittgenstein's thinking sprang from the modern development of mathematical logic, and so it did. But this tells us nothing about why his thought went so far away from this. Although the seeds are there in the *Tractatus* (i.e., the "mystical"), this is often ignored. Anscombe gives us a short biographical sketch and reports that Wittgenstein had read Schopenhauer by the age of sixteen. Wittgenstein became interested in Frege, and we know that Frege had no concern with ethics but worked purely with logic and the foundations of mathematics.

How did Wittgenstein get so far away from Frege's concerns, and Russell's too? Or for that matter, why did his strong and important friendship with Bertrand Russell degenerate into such distance? If Wittgenstein's work explains this (and there are clues, as we have pointed out), it does so only by using his biography to illuminate it. For one thing, "Russell was thoroughly imbued with the tradition of British

---

[1] Harper & Row, 2nd ed., New York, 1965.

empiricism. Wittgenstein's admirers have generally been like Russell in this, and have assumed Wittgenstein was too" (p. 14). Therefore, many interpreters have philosophical assumptions quite out of tune with the *Tractatus*. Remember: (1) neither Frege nor Russell claimed to understand it; and (2) Wittgenstein was notoriously uncomplimentary about British philosophy.

Yet without the developments in logic by Frege and Russell, "it is inconceivable that Wittgenstein should have written the *Tractatus*" (p. 16). Thus, it must be that Wittgenstein's intent for philosophy, whether fully explicit at this time or not, goes far beyond Frege and Russell's. Logic and mathematics were used by Wittgenstein as tools to achieve a different purpose. But these proved to be inadequate and even a frustration, so he moved beyond them. True, Russell began to write "popular" philosophical works, but they represented "British Clarity" all the while Wittgenstein is moving toward monkhood and silence.

The principle theme of the *Tractatus*, Anscombe reports, "is the connection between language, or thought, and reality." "Sentences, or their mental counterparts, are pictures of facts. Only we must not suppose that which is pictured by a proposition has to exist" (p. 19). But if Wittgenstein wants to "get to 'reality'," as is clear, logic first and eventually language may prove to be inadequate vehicles. The *Tractatus* already contains its own severe qualification: "There is indeed much that is inexpressible—which we must not try to state, but must contemplate without words" (p. 19). If true, what must we do to make this contemplation successful? Surely the first thing is not to let language confuse us. But our goal is never language for its own sake. We know that its revelatory powers are limited.

Anscombe cites Karl Popper's characterization of the *Tractatus* and remarks that "there is a great deal about 'observation' in Popper's account, and very little about it in the *Tractatus*" (p. 26). It was hard for Cambridge, and particularly for Oxford, not to see Wittgenstein in terms of empiricism, even though he begins and ends far from it. "Whatever elementary propositions may be, they are not simple observational statements," Anscombe concludes (p. 27). There is hardly any epistemology (that British obsession) in the *Tractatus*, and "Wittgenstein evidently did not think that epistemology had any bearing on his subject matter" (p. 27). The theory of knowledge is in the philosophy of psychology, as a Positivist might have said.

Anscombe reports that Wittgenstein was convinced that he had "penetrated the essential nature of truth, falsehood and negation with his picture theory" (p. 79). The residue that would not fit in were attempts to say the inexpressible. When this is sometimes called the "nonsensical," it should be remembered that this is so only according to the rigorous internal criteria of the *Tractatus*. All "beyond the picture theory" was never declared to be non-existent and certainly not unimportant. Wittgenstein and Frege both avoided making theory of knowledge the cardinal theme of philosophy, but Logical Positivism stressed verification "and theory of knowledge once more reigned supreme" (p. 152). "We can see how the *Tractatus* generated Logical Positivism, although the two philosophies are incompatible" (p. 152).

The *Tractatus* says that I determine the sense of a proposition by determining in what circumstances I could call it true (4.063). "There is no room for criticizing a sentence on the grounds that we have not stipulated what situation it describes; but only on the ground that we have not assigned a reference to some of the words in it" (p. 154). Knowledge and certainty are topics for philosophy of logic, and Wittgenstein is concerned with these. "But logical theory must allow for the certainty of propositions which are not logically necessary" (p. 155). There is reason to doubt some parts of Wittgenstein's own later criticism of the *Tractatus* in the *Investigations*.

The cardinal problem of philosophy, Wittgenstein told Russell, is the theory of what can be expressed by propositions, i.e., by language, and what cannot be expressed by propositions by can only be shown (p. 161). Which of the possibilities is actual has to be discovered by comparing the propositions with reality. It cannot be settled whether the proposition is true or false just by considering what it means. Philosophy cannot be confined within logic or language when in fact its whole meaning comes in its comparison with "reality." "Now the things that would be true if they could be said are obviously important," Anscombe concludes (p. 162). But logic cannot be thought of as something independent of the world either.

"The idea of the world as having *limits* which philosophy displays to us appears over and over again in the *Tractatus*" (p. 169). "The feeling of the world as a limited whole is the mystical feeling" (p. 169). Wittgenstein states: "We feel that even if all *possible* scientific questions have been answered, still the problems of life have not been touched at all" (p. 170, T.6.52). Certainly this proved true in his own life post-*Tractatus*. "The meaning of the world must lie outside the world" (6.41). Thus God does not, and for the *Tractatus* could not, reveal himself in the world (T.6.432). Thus, the will that is the bearer of the ethical (T.6.423) belongs among the transcendentals of the *Tractatus,* along with the mystical and the meaning of life, Anscombe concludes (p. 171).

Having said this, Anscombe goes on to say that it is this part of the *Tractatus* which seems "most obviously wrong" (p. 171). That is quite possible, but it is also quite true that both Wittgenstein's post-*Tractatus* philosophy and his life are spent struggling with all that lies outside the *Tractatus*'s technical structure and that this may account for his subsequent troubled biography and professional dissatisfaction. His work reflects his final judgment on the *Tractatus:* it shows how little has been done when these problems have been solved. How early he realized this it is hard to say. But for all his recognized work in logic, still the centers of his concern and of the source of meaning in his personal and in his professional life did not really lie there. The *Tractatus* can be called a language game, rightfully so.

Turning to Norman Malcolm's *Ludwig Wittgenstein: A Memoir,*[2] we have something quite different, not a technical restructuring and elucidation but a biographical sketch by G.H. von Wright and Malcolm's personal memoir. If we want to try to determine from studying Wittgenstein's life what forced him out of the "security" constructed in the logical system of the *Tractatus* and into an odyssey that seemed to lead to a labyrinth, we need that contrast if we are to understand the later writings and his increasingly restless lifestyle.

He was admittedly eccentric in personal behavior, but one might not think that relevant for a logician. This only brings to light the question of whether logic and mathematics were Wittgenstein's "fly bottle," which in a real sense the *Tractatus* had put him in, while it still contained "the mystical" as an escape clause from the system of final truth. The structure constructed to solve all philosophical problems had a genuine Achilles' heel. It admittedly left out most of what was personally (and increasingly philosophically) important to Wittgenstein. But the fly could not release itself. The struggle and the wandering began.

Von Wright is as close an observer of Wittgenstein as Anscombe, and his introduction tells us that "Wittgenstein inspired two important schools of thought, both of which he repudiated," Logical Positivism and linguistic philosophy (p. 1). Given the confines imposed on philosophy by these movements, it is easy to see how they could not contain Wittgenstein's interests or his restlessness. We get a hint of this when we realize that "he did not participate in the world-wide discussion to

---

[2] Oxford University Press, London, 1958, 1962.

which his work and thought gave rise" (p. 1). One needs to understand something of Wittgenstein's life in order to see why this might be true, since the ordinary human response is to respond to the flattery of attention. His eyes were focused somewhere else, and we need to see where, if we can. Or did he really know what he sought, in detail, except that academic discussions did not fulfill his quest? In fact, he finally rejected that life.

Von Wright comments: "It is probably true that he lived on the border of mental illness. A fear of being driven across it followed him all his life" (p. 3). But can we understand what the fear is that might have driven him? Surely not logic or mathematics. But perhaps it was the confines of language which held him from saying directly all that was important, plus his own strictures on what can be expressed. What language does not, cannot, say may be personally most important, and Wittgenstein lives out the contradiction of having set those strict limits while still yearning to move beyond them. And he did not read only logic. He read Tolstoy who led him to the Gospels. He had read Schopenhauer's *World as Will and Idea* early on, but what may be most significant is that his rooms are often described as a "monk's cell."

He contemplated entering a monastery but did not. He felt unable to satisfy the inner conditions of monastic life. Why? He had established conditions which made it impossible to express in his lifestyle what he found important. The early Wittgenstein learned from Frege and Russell, but the later Wittgenstein, von Wright comments, "has no ancestors in the history of thought" (p. 15). This could be no more than partially true. We must consider whether, in the rigorous spiritual struggle which expressed itself outwardly again and again, Wittgenstein had a host of ancestors but was not in a position to follow their lead. His lectures were even highly unacademic, so it could not have been the role of a professor he sought. He often went to live in seclusion, as spiritual pilgrims do.

Another contradiction: he avoided making acquaintances but needed and sought friends. Yet at the same time he might later distance himself from them. Von Wright says: "I believe that most of those who loved him and had his friendship also feared him" (p. 18). He continues: there are two forms of seriousness of character. "One is fixed in 'strong principles'; the other springs from a passionate heart. The former has to do with morality and the latter, I believe, is closer to religion" (p. 19). "The thought of God, he said, was above all for him the thought of the fearful judge" (p. 20). "God" had been ruled out of discourse in the

Tractatus, but the fearful judge was a moving force in Wittgenstein's life.

"His life was a constant journey, and doubt was the moving force within him" (p. 20). Knowledge was for him immediately connected to doing. Yet as a logician/professor he could not "do" what his earnestness and severity drove him to. He received deeper impressions from writers in the borderland between philosophy, religion, and poetry, more than from philosophers (in the restricted sense). He read Augustine, Kierkegaard, Dostoyevsky and Tolstoy. But perhaps more important for our perspective, von Wright comments: "The philosophical sections of St. Augustine's *Confessions* show a strong resemblance to Wittgenstein's own way of doing philosophy" (p. 21). However, the *Tractatus* does not fit the confessional mode.

He was at once a logician and a mystic. It might be time, then, as his life becomes clear to us, to consider "the mystic" as just as much a key to Wittgenstein's work as others have in the past stressed "the logician." Von Wright concludes his insightful introduction: "What makes a man's work *classic* is often just this multiplicity, which invites and at the same time resists our craving for clearer understanding" (p. 22). If so, we cannot expect his work to clear up all philosophical problems, either in the sense of the rigor of the *Tractatus* or in the more vague and amorphous style of the *Investigations* and beyond. True, Wittgenstein may have claimed to have discovered a new method in philosophy. But given these paradoxical factors, philosophy returns to the classical mold of raising questions rather than answering them. Our problems may become more clear, but they are not thereby solved.

Contrary to superficial understanding, increased clarity does not make questions go away. Quite the opposite. They intensify as we see more distinctly what we are up against, what an earlier "ignorance" hid from us. This surely is true in Wittgenstein's life. The pressure mounted rather than relaxed, in spite of all that he had accomplished. It cannot possibly be said that philosophy now dissolved into questions of logic and grammar and language, since it did not do that for Wittgenstein himself.

Malcolm's memoir is not as interpretive as von Wright's introduction. But it gives a good picture of Wittgenstein, particularly in his later years, since he came to stay with the Malcolms in Ithaca. In 1938, when Malcolm first heard Wittgenstein lecture, he admits that he understood "almost nothing of the lectures, until I re-studied my notes approximately ten years later" (p. 23). But these lectures were given without preparation and without notes. "His whole personality was commanding, even imperial" (p. 24). In a plain wooden chair in his spare room, "he carried on a visible struggle with his thoughts" (p. 26). The meetings consisted mainly of dialogue, but often with prolonged periods of silence. "Wittgenstein was a frightening person at these classes" (p. 27). He worked with himself to achieve complete understanding.

"What made him an awesome and even terrible person, both as a teacher and in personal relationships, was his ruthless integrity, which did not spare himself or anyone else" (p. 27). So his philosophy after the *Tractatus* denied him the certainty he continued to seek and his integrity denied him the love of friends he continued to need. Many students dropped out, "because they found the material unintelligible or uninteresting" (p. 29). Yet still he said that philosophical work might be a matter consisting entirely of jokes or of questions without answers. He tried to persuade Malcolm to "give up philosophy and become a ranch-hand." "He had an abhorrence of academic life... and of the life of the professional philosopher" (p. 30).

An honest and serious person could not be a university teacher, be believed (p. 30). Yet he continued on in philosophy and in teaching too for a time. Malcolm reports: "He was constantly depressed, I think, by the impossibility of arriving at understanding in philosophy" (p. 32). "Often as we walked together he would stop and exclaim 'Oh, my God!', looking at me almost piteously, as if imploring a divine intervention in human events" (p. 32). Yet a casual remark of Malcolm's about British "national character" made Wittgenstein so mad that he stopped taking his walks with Malcolm and kept the incident in his mind for years. He evidently had as much trouble forgiving others as he had in forgiving himself.

Yet when Malcolm wrote later about leaving teaching at Princeton to go into the Navy, Wittgenstein replied: "I wish you could live quietly, and be in a position to be kind and *understanding* to all sorts of human beings who *need* it! Because we all need this sort of thing very badly" (p. 37). The struggle between simplicity and high intelligence never ceased, just as Thomas Merton always struggled over the special privileges his position as a writer brought to him vs. the austere life of his fellow Trappists. Yet philosophy still gave Wittgenstein his only satisfaction, he reports (p. 38). He constantly reported his feeling of loneliness. What is the use of studying philosophy, he concluded, "if it does not make you more conscientious..." (p. 39).

Monk subtitles his biography of Wittgenstein, "The duty of genius." But Wittgenstein himself remarks: "You see, I know it is difficult to think *well* about 'certainty,' 'probability,' 'perception,' etc. But it is, if possible, still more difficult to think, or *try* to think, really honestly about your life and other people's lives" (p. 39). Genius has its burdens and its paradoxes too. When Malcolm finally got back to England after corresponding with Wittgenstein, he reports the meeting as "difficult." "He showed me no cordiality at all" (p. 40). "We sat in silence for a long time" (p. 40). Clearly Wittgenstein fought constantly with himself over friendships, his treatment of other people, and also with his professional life. He wanted to "resign the absurd job of a professor of philosophy. It's a kind of living death" (p. 47).

He intended to introduce novelty into philosophy. "What I give is the morphology of the use of an expression. I show that it has kinds of uses of which you had not dreamed" (p. 50). "What I do is to suggest, or even invent, other ways of looking at it" (p. 50). This may relieve your mental cramp, as he explains, but assuredly it is not certainty producing. Like Kierkegaard, he hoped for at least one person who would understand his book when published (the *Investigations*). Peter Geach once remarked that gatherings in Wittgenstein's room "had the appearance of a Quaker prayer meeting" (p. 53). Quakers use silence for instruction, and so did Wittgenstein.

He stressed the necessity to suffer in order to create insight, in a manner not unlike Kierkegaard. "The measure of a man's greatness would be in terms of what his work *cost* him" (p. 55). He always considered an issue in terms of what his duty was. He always lived in obscurity, "discouraging all attempts to make him into a celebrity or public figure" (p. 59). Yet he said: "Although I cannot *give* affection, I have great *need* for it" (p. 61). Human kindness, human concern was for him far more important than intellectual power. Yet friendly relationships with him were difficult. He felt himself to be a failure as a teacher.

During the First World War he read Tolstoy on religion, which made a great impression. No believer of orthodoxy, he said "he thought he could understand the conception of God, in so far as it is involved in one's awareness of one's own sin and guilt" (pp. 70-71). Religious judgment, forgiveness, and redemption, Malcolm believes, had some intelligibility for Wittgenstein, "as being related in his mind to feelings of disgust with himself, in intense desire for purity, and in a sense of the helplessness of human beings to make themselves better" (p. 71). Every novice master in a monastery would recognize this as the attitude which brings the serious penitent to try the monastic life. Wittgenstein could comprehend a judging, redeeming God, but not intellectual "proofs" for God.

Wittgenstein read Augustine, as well as Tolstoy. He found Kierkegaard a "really religious man," and George Fox, the English Quaker, he thought to be a practical religious man whose approach was not intellectual/rational. Malcolm concludes: I think there was for him the possibility of religion. This was as a "form of life" in which he did not participate, but with which he was sympathetic and interested. "I suspect that he regarded religious belief as based on qualities of character and will that he himself did not possess" (p. 72). "I'd like to be alone somewhere," Wittgenstein wrote to Malcolm, "I need a longish spell of thinking *alone*, without having to talk to anybody." He could have accepted the Trappist lifestyle, but his self-appraisal did not allow it.

Kierkegaard's *Works of Love* impressed him, perhaps because love was so difficult for him to give. Though he said it did not have the good effects on him it would have on "deeper souls" (p. 75). "What warms my heart most is human kindness" (p. 80); but he found little of this, especially in living alone. Still, Malcolm reports one remark that struck him most of all as summing up a good deal of Wittgenstein's philosophy. It was: "An expression has meaning only in the stream of life" (p. 93). So one might take all of his later writings as an attempt to take his work in logic and to put them "into the stream of life." But he was not an Existentialist like Kierkegaard, and such an attempt could not bring him satisfaction. For that matter, Kierkegaard did not succeed in achieving personal reconciliation either.

One of Wittgenstein's last remarks Malcolm finds mysterious and strangely moving: "Tell them I've had a wonderful life!" (p. 98). Why? Malcolm reports: because of "his profound pessimism, the intensity of his mental and moral suffering, his need for love together with his harshness that repelled love" (p. 98). Wittgenstein was a model candidate for religious conversion but could never experience it. He could not forgive himself, and he could never, as he thought others had, experience God as offering him forgiveness and reconciliation in unmerited love. Wittgenstein's rocky friendship with Russell, to whom he owed so much, indicates some of this conflict. Moore, on the other hand, possessed some of the human qualities he admired.[3]

Von Wright comments that Wittgenstein had a deep affection and respect for Moore, "in spite of the fundamental dissimilarity of the two men's personality and thinking" (p. 4). So Wittgenstein cannot have taken intellectual agreement as primary in his personal relations. Perhaps he saw in Moore some of the common humanity he prized in the ordinary folk he sometimes lived among. But his friendship with Russell came first and it was important. Wittgenstein once ended a letter by saying: "Logic is a very good invention," (p. 18) which indicates its non-humanness, and his friendship with Russell was largely based on logic.

"I will always be yours," he ends one letter written to Russell from his cabin in Norway (p. 28), but it did not prove to be true. Yet he begged Russell to write to him. He ends another letter, which we cannot dismiss as total irony: "Pray for me and God bless you! (If there is such a thing)" (p. 34). He stands outside religion looking in the window. Yet he loved isolation too, creating his own paradox. "Being alone here does me no end of good and I do not think I could bear life among people" (p. 43). And he finally tells Russell that he has come to the conclusion "that we really don't suit one another," (p. 50) thus rejecting an important friendship. He tells Russell that their ideas are totally different so that "there cannot be any real relation of friendship between us" (p. 50). Yet he knew that friendship is not primarily intellectual.

Wittgenstein craves love and yet claims that his ideas flow when he is in isolation. "My life has been one nasty mess so far," he tells us, "but need that go on indefinitely?", he asks. Perhaps he answers his own question when he reports a deep perpetual seething inside and asks, "How can I be a logician before I'm a human being? For the most important thing is to settle accounts with myself!" (p. 58). This he never did, nor did he settle the conflict between his logic and his humanity. Russell comments that "he has become a complete mystic" (p. 82). The difficult truth is that he never gave up being a logician and yet could not become a mystic either.

---

[3] Wittgenstein, *Letters to Russell, Keynes and Moore*, ed. von Wright, Cornell University Press, Ithaca, 1974.

B. MONK: LIFE AT THE BORDER

We have already used a great many insights from Ray Monk's impressive biography.[4] The context Monk has given us makes it possible to draw out points in Wittgenstein's writings which might otherwise be passed over as miscellaneous. With the framework of the life before us, the work takes on different meanings. Our task now is to cite some of the insights Monk's work provides. But first it may be helpful to outline the thesis which has been gradually emerging. It is correct to say "gradually emerging," since given the technical complexity of Wittgenstein's work, it would be impossible to uncover any thesis before working your way through a general review, as we have just done.

The thesis is: (1) it is not possible to account for the radical changes in Wittgenstein's professional views without the context of his life. And: (2) it is not possible to comprehend the upheavals and struggles which dominate his life without seeing how they come about due to the views he put forward and the way in which these either blocked, or at least make exceedingly difficult, the goals and concerns which increasingly dominated his life. These "concerns" were present at the beginning of his professional career, but they became accentuated into crisis as it becomes clear that his own restrictions block the expression of what is most meaningful in his life.

Remember: one dominant theme, with which many agree, is that it is not possible to offer a final synthesis or even a distillation of Wittgenstein's writings taken as a whole, including the journals. Still, we are led to argue, this is not wholly due to technical developments as he works away from the early doctrine. These changes could have been handled in "less radical" ways as Wittgenstein evolves. Thus, the shape of his emerging themes reflects his struggle to fit his personal concerns within the early framework he erected. And in particular: what he is trying to tell us about "philosophy" specifically may be misunderstood without the setting of his biography. To use biography as a key is acceptable for Existentialism. Does it fit Wittgenstein?

It is now fully agreed that for all the logical, technical rigor in the *Tractatus*, it is set in the context of "mysticism." That which cannot be said clearly is not abandoned. It is left as important but "beyond philosophy" as this had been developed. The notion that one "abandons" all that has lead the reader through the propositions of the *Tractatus* is quite consistent with any number of "meditative,"

---

[4] *Ludwig Wittgenstein: The Duty of Genius*, Free Press, New York, 1990.

"contemplative" ways that instill discipline for the purpose of seeking "enlightenment." Once insight is achieved, one no longer has need of the guide or of the arduous procedures. Yet Wittgenstein goes beyond his self-imposed restrictions. Why? Because what increasingly concerns him must be expressed, and yet the "system" does not allow it.

We know what a major role aesthetics played in his life, particularly music. He liked musical examples, and they must be given "meaning." He rejected the Logical Positivists' exclusions and their attempts to keep philosophy pure and rigorous. Thus, it is his person, not so much the early work itself, which forces upon him the task of radically altering his views of philosophy. However perhaps more important, his early reading of Schopenhauer, although never followed up explicitly, plus his admiration for Augustine's *Confessions*, James' *Varieties of Religious Experience*, together with his reading of Kierkegaard and Tolstoy (who will be considered separately), all increased his concern with religion rather than lessened it. He adopted a monk-like lifestyle: simplicity, poverty, isolation, silence. But since he could never commit himself, this lifestyle in many ways blocked its own expression.

Many, then, could live a life satisfying in itself without involving it in their professional work. Logicians, mathematicians have been "religious," but this need not show itself in their work. One is a satisfied teacher and fulfills himself/herself in that way, irregardless of professional success. Wittgenstein was immensely successful professionally, yet rather than enjoy it, this increasingly made him uncomfortable and eventually led him to abandon it. Something in the personal goal he pursued led him toward a life quite different from that of the scholar and academic. However, he never found that fulfillment personally either.

How do these biographical matters affect his professional work? The logical structure of the *Tractatus* embodies the finality he sought, supposedly the release from endless philosophical wandering. But it is a "fly bottle" holding Wittgenstein inside looking out at the "mystical." He is able to see all of value, the ethical/religious, but he is not able to touch it or even to express it, given the confines of philosophy which at this point are identical with his stated logical structure. Language is essentially confined to propositional structure. As the *Tractatus* is debated and as the discussion with Frege, Russell, and the Vienna Circle continues, Wittgenstein has gone through his Army, his prisoner of war experience, and he then works as a rural elementary teacher and as a monastery gardener.

In his wanderings, seeking isolation and friendship simultaneously, the inner needs pressing upon him for expression break out of the fly bottle by splitting the rigid, precise structure of the "bottle" into isolated bits. Language, in the sense of logical structure, could not "do the job," elegant as it might be. But in "smashing the bottle," precise structure goes too, and Wittgenstein the logician sees no possible "structure" for philosophy other than that. Language, once beautifully captured in a glass cage itself, now becomes more rich and various as it fragments. But it still cannot develop the power needed to give expression to Wittgenstein's needs.

Turning inward to the mind, to "experience," we get the psychology of color and the analyses of feeling and perception. These are subtle, interior in a sense, full of nuance But these remarks never gather enough structure to move beyond individual analysis. The logical framework of the *Tractatus* had produced "mental cramps" in philosophy, and he could remove these because they came as the result of the "system" Wittgenstein erected (as would be the case for any constructed system). Yet in the *Tractatus* Wittgenstein is seriously interested in the relationship of logic/language to "reality" such that truth is captured. But if the "system" is rejected, then without that mechanism is he driven towards "solipsism" (which he rejects) and to seeing "reality" in psychological terms?

Wittgenstein's later life could not be satisfying, once out of that fly bottle, because his personal needs could even less be expressed by "ordinary language." Kierkegaard could be unsystematic and reach conviction by passion, as Wittgenstein noted. But Wittgenstein was unable to commit his intelligence that far, a block Kierkegaard often remarked on. Professional life and teaching could have been made into vehicles for expression; they might have been a sufficient outlet. But these were pedantic compared to the stringent routine the monk seeks to impose upon himself. And the "new method" for relieving philosophical problems by the analysis of language ironically moved philosophy more distant from Wittgenstein's increasing internal pressures.

Can Wittgenstein's "philosophical moves" be accounted for without resorting to biography? His remarks on mathematics continue throughout his life. They force no philosophical revolution. The *Tractatus* has points which are open to debate. But these might be "repaired" instead of faulting the whole structure. Specifically, why not join the Vienna Circle, or league with Russell and Frege, his two original mentors? Contact with the positivism of the Circle convinced

Wittgenstein early on, despite what seems like their parallel projects, that he rebels (at least subconsciously) against restricting philosophy. He finds so much of importance that he cannot discuss with them and yet must consider. If the *Tractatus* had provided the "enlightenment" that made its ladder now dispensable, thought should not rebel.

In spite of disagreements with Frege and Russell's widely diverging philosophical interests, why not continue in that circle, holding lively debates in British academic circles, working to spread out from the *Tractatus*? Instead, the entire academic/teaching life becomes distasteful and unsatisfying to him. Nothing about the *Tractatus* demands philosophy as an ascetic practice, which it increasingly becomes for him. The monk's search and exploration of isolation does, although it also tends to move beyond logic and verbal expression into a rigorous style of life, Spartan in order to "cleanse the mind" (and soul). It is this inner search that Wittgenstein's revolution in philosophy comes to reflect, not merely a modification of "errors" in the *Tractatus*.

In particular, what accounts for Wittgenstein's increasing "pragmatism," his insistence that verbalization (intellection) is meaningless unless embodied in act? More must now be "shown," because the *Tractatus* has placed so much in the "mystical" beyond logical language, and how better to "show" this than by practice, by embodiment? The picture theory is an attempt to let words do what the *Tractatus* restricted them from. And it is an "odd" theory, although we talk of "word pictures," it is true. But Wittgenstein has previously excluded all that falls outside technical/logical language. "Universals" we know are not visualizable and belong to the realm which Plato said the mind attends to without using the senses. So "family resemblance" is a "weak" way to get universal conceptions into the discourse.

The monk's life may be seen as the attempt to give the inner spirit an outer expression, to form a picture of what is not easily expressed. In all religious/meditative disciplines isolation has always been used as a technique, not only to strengthen the inner spirit, but to find words emerging from silence that may at least partially express what ordinary language cannot do. And how odd that Wittgenstein turns to ordinary language (except that it is away from logic) when the spiritual rigors he places on himself, the isolation and silence he undergoes all the while seeking love, are ancient techniques for producing esoteric expression. His life moves to the esoteric; his formal thought to the ordinary.

Now, let us see what "validation" the biography Monk has written can give to the thesis that only Wittgenstein's life can account for the shifts in his philosophical thought. First, Monk remarks that the professional fascination with Wittgenstein goes beyond the influence which his philosophy has had (p. xvii). He wanted to overcome himself, a transformation that would make philosophy unnecessary (p. 4). But since he did not do that, we must take the aim to eliminate philosophy as unrealized. Or, we could consider this as like the Zen monk who does not need to speak about enlightenment once it is experienced. However, in distinction, Western mystics have tended to feel the compulsion to speak, even though their words are inadequate to their experience. Wittgenstein lies in between, seeking to make philosophical thought unnecessary, resisting direct expression but still continuing to speak.

Like Kierkegaard, Wittgenstein's family saw him as a contented boy, while he describes his childhood as unhappy. Kierkegaard describes this as an inner suffering even though the external life was stable. But the language of logic is not adaptable to express inner anguish. Wittgenstein was born into a religious faith, which he quite early lost; Kierkegaard lived in the middle of religious faith which he found too easy to accept. If philosophical thinking for Wittgenstein began with painful contradictions and seeks to resolve these, replacing confusion with clarity (p. 26), we can see the contradictions in his life: his attempt to resolve them vs. the new method to achieve clarity. One cannot fail to see the opposite of resolution in Wittgenstein's own life.

As early as the years he went to Manchester to study aeronautics, Wittgenstein describes his physical and emotional isolation "and his deep need for a close companion" (p. 29). He never overcame this. He had a few close companions, but none that stayed to remove isolation permanently. When Wittgenstein studies with Russell later, he is described as "full of boiling passion which may drive him anywhere" (p. 43). He has the disposition of an artist, intuitive and moody," (p. 43) all of which is not likely to find expression in mathematical logic. His morality was based on integrity and duty, important to him but "out of bounds" for the *Tractatus* to express. He had a rigorously logical mind and an impulsive and obsessional nature, Russell says (p. 47). This is the quality of genius, Russell thought, but it is hard to confine to either logic or isolation.

Out of suicidal loneliness and suffering, Russell's encouragement to pursue philosophy had been his "salvation" (p. 50). He told Russell that he admired the text, "what shall it profit a man if gain the whole world and lose his own soul," and this involved suffering and the power to endure it (p. 51). Those words of Jesus could easily be the motto of

Wittgenstein's life and work. He gained the world but he never ceased to live as a lost soul, almost literally giving away the world as it came to him, continually suffering, but unaware that gaining one's soul depends more on giving love (in Jesus words) than in seeking it or in enduring suffering.

He told Malcolm that the Stoic thought of being independent of fate and circumstances made him see for the first time "the possibility of religion" (p. 51). The feeling of being absolutely safe he thought paradigmatic of religious experience, and he read James' *Varieties of Religious Experience* with approval. The problem is that for the Christian context, which Wittgenstein inherits, feeling "safe" is the result of belief. This Wittgenstein respects but could not commit himself to. And "grace" is God's gift, not an individual accomplishment as it is for the Stoic. Thus Wittgenstein was blocked from the Christian experience of being "saved" or of knowing God in the experience of receiving a gift (grace).

Wittgenstein was told by Russel that he thought "too much about himself" (p. 65). This brings to mind a prominent Gospel theme which Wittgenstein never referred to in our written record and certainly did not seem to understand as he understood many of Jesus' words clearly: "He who seeks to save his life shall lose it, while he who loses his life..." Wittgenstein can be seen as constantly involved in an intense battle to "save" himself, both intellectually and personally. But he was never able to release his intense self concentration, thus frustrating his personal life and his professional life. If we accept his later claim to have evolved a method that dissolves philosophical mental cramps, we know this involves shifting focus away from "the mystical" to the simple, all the while leaving what is most important unexpressed.

Wittgenstein had remarked that "religious experience consisted in getting rid of worry" (p. 67). Sympathetic as he was to such a lived event, it must be clear that Wittgenstein never himself experienced this, in spite of its desirability. If Wittgenstein actually thought that "the possibility of greatness, therefore, demands a separation from the loved one," (p. 90) it might explain why he would leave Cambridge. He needs love but separation from physical proximity is needed to preserve it. Thus we see the struggle between greatness and love (in the form of desire) which leads him to isolation in Norway. Had he seen love as a gift, a giving, a grace, would his obsession for greatness have driven him to isolation; and would he have seen love as demanding separation in order to preserve it, an odd notion and one that haunts him?

If "philosophy gives no picture of reality," (p. 92) how is one to get in touch with "reality" and express it if one feels driven to do so? The silence of isolation in Norway is the mystic/monk's classical setting, but what does one do if in silence "reality" should become clearer? The year in Skjolden was "possibly the most productive of his life," Monk reports (p. 94). Complete clarity or death, was his motto, but what if what one is driven to express does not admit of, or actually defies, clarity? "He was forced to realize that, however close he might be to complete, uncompromising clarity in the field of logic, he was as far away from it as ever in his personal life—in himself" (p. 97). And yet his "pragmatic" turn forces him to seek embodiment, a change in life, an expression for passion.

William James had commented on the spiritual value of facing death heroically, and this might offer some explanation of Wittgenstein's not only service in the Army in World War I but his actually seeking dangerous duty. "Perhaps the nearness to death will bring light into life. God enlighten me," he wrote (p. 112). He wanted a transformation, and from the war he wanted his personality to be "born again," as the New Testament puts it. But valuable as the war, and eventually the prison, experience may have been, such personal transformation ("salvation"?) eludes Wittgenstein all his life, just as his goal of completing philosophy, and thus easing mental pains, does too.

"I think of suicide," he reports, but what saved him from suicide was not the war experience itself but his finding and being captivated by Tolstoy's *Gospel in Brief* (p. 115). The book fascinated him. It became a talisman. "He carried it wherever he went, and read it so often that he came to know whole passages by heart. He became known to his comrades as "the man with the gospels"" (p. 116). At least for a time, he was not only a believer but an evangelist, recommending Tolstoy's *Gospels* to anyone in distress. Thus the project, and the paradox, of his life is set: combining logical theory with religious mysticism. From this bottle the fly escapes only with death.

The spiritual sustenance of Tolstoy's *Gospels* kept him alive. It allowed him to lighten his external appearance "so as to leave undisturbed my inner being" (p. 116). His ideal: that whatever happened "externally," nothing could happen to *him*, that is to his innermost being. His diary contains repeated exhortations to God to help him not to lose himself. But in spite of the obvious profoundness of this war-time experience, can we understand Wittgenstein's later life and his work as a still constant attempt to prevent losing himself and an attempt to "save himself" in spite of Jesus' advice in the gospels against trying to do so? This was accompanied by the constant disturbance of his "inner being," in spite of the thought that this could not happen.

But for him sensuality and philosophical thought were inextricably linked (p. 117). He said: "Don't be dependent on the external world and then you have no fear of what happens in it" (p. 116). Yet sensuality is inextricably bound to the external world, so that its link to philosophical thought binds him to it, too, as intellectual acknowledgment and the need for love also do. Thus, his soul could not, as he hoped, "inhabit an entirely different realm" (p. 116). His isolation was an attempt to separate himself from the "crude, stupid, and malicious." But both love and the intellectual life kept him bound to it so that his soul could not inhabit "an entirely different realm."

He believes there must be a logical structure in common between a proposition and a state of affairs, and this commonalty of structure enables language to represent reality (p. 118). There could hardly be an assumption more crucial to Wittgenstein's project. But the problem is: what if the "common structure" is purely formal and as such misses all that is concrete (and possibly non-logical) about reality? If so, then the path to certainty, first set out in the answers of the *Tractatus* and then in the method for "solving" philosophical problems in the *Investigations*, doubles back upon itself and yields the certainty of logical/linguistic structure but misses what is important in reality?

It is clear that some of Wittgenstein's "happiness" is tied up with the success of both of these approaches, but he also continued to believe that "Christianity is the only *sure* way to happiness" (p. 122). It is not a matter of whether Christianity is "true." That has to do with logical structure and picturing. The question is whether it offers some help in dealing with an unbearable and otherwise meaningless existence. And here he follows William James: this is not a matter of belief but of practice, a way of living. "Only Christian *practice*, a life such as he who died on the Cross *lived*, is Christian," Wittgenstein states (p. 122). His theme: the essence of religion lies in feeling and in practice (p. 123).

If we compare the view of happiness and religion with the hope that the logical structure of propositions would picture reality, we see even more clearly how much logical structure will miss what is important about reality for Wittgenstein. That cannot be pictured in propositions but in feeling and in act. And as ordinary language picturing the world replaces propositions, we are a little closer to aspects of reality which propositions may miss, because we are also into the vagueness of much speech and human behavior. Yet religion and ethics are still not captured there. As already mentioned, Wittgenstein said that Tolstoy's *Gospels* "virtually kept me alive" (p. 132) at one time. And he literally knew whole passages of *The Brothers Karamazov* by heart.

During his time as a soldier in the front lines of battle, he said: "Perhaps the nearness of death will bring the light of life" (p. 138). This is a far cry from the "enlightenment" of either the *Tractatus* or the *Investigations* and is sought in a quite different manner. He asks himself what he knows about God and the purpose of life. "The meaning of life, i.e. the meaning of the world, we can call God" (p.141). Such sentences are shut out of significant meaning in the *Tractatus* and clarified so as to remove mental cramps in the *Investigations* (although such puzzles are not much considered). But there are things which cannot be put into words, showing vs. saying. They are the mystical and Wittgenstein concentrated much of his attention here.

A close friend of Wittgenstein's, with whom he shared his experience of religious awakening, described him as a person who "suffered acutely under the discrepancy between the world as it is and as it ought to be" (p. 149). If the *Tractatus* represents the world as it ought to be, and if the *Investigations* reflects a little more of the world as it is, there is still a great deal of the world outside of language games. Logic and mysticism sprung from the same root in the *Tractatus*. The link is "the idea of the unutterable truth that makes itself manifest" (p. 130). Speaking of poetry he said: "If only you do not try to utter what is unutterable then *nothing* gets lost. But the unutterable will be—unutterably—contained in what has been uttered" (p. 151).

The nonsense that results from trying "to say what only can be shown is not only logically untenable but ethically undesirable" (p. 156). This must be enacted in altered modes of life. Of course, Russell's insistence on the applicability of meta-languages abolished the sphere of the mystical, while Wittgenstein's insistence on the impossibility of saying what can only be shown preserves it (p. 166). The hardship suffered during the war had changed Wittgenstein, and it was the very thing that gave his life meaning. This stands in ironic contrast to the finality claims of the *Tractatus*, or perhaps more accurately it indicates a divorce between logical clarity and meaning. He is driven to philosophical thought, but what he liked best in mysticism was "its power to make him stop thinking" (p. 183)—that noted virtue of silence.

Commenting on a friend's summary of Christian belief, Wittgenstein says: "Even if their most perfect expression should turn out to be silence, then they are nonetheless true" (p. 186). It can still be quite "true" that what one cannot speak about one must remain silent (T.7). But it is also the case that the criteria for truth in the *Tractatus* and the *Investigations* are still specialized and restricted and could not convey the whole meaning of truth. Wittgenstein spent a summer working as a gardener in a monastery near Vienna. He was "outside looking in," so to speak. But: "External causes of suffering continued to confine Wittgenstein to the 'world of the unhappy man'" (p. 191). This, you may recall, was defined by Kierkegaard as the man whose present life was empty.

If that which was not said in the *Tractatus* turned out to be more important to him than what he had said (p. 243), the philosophical life can be seen as a way of "showing" what cannot be expressed. However, the contradiction is bound to surface: "Not only does Wittgenstein talk of those things, about which he insists one must be silent; he dominates *all* talk of them" (p. 257). To understand this one must study the classic mystics. All assert the unsayability but then write a great deal about their experiences. Wittgenstein, however, faced an almost intolerable burden, just because he had a more rigorous technical definition of what can be said.

The *Tractatus* deals with language in isolation; "The *Investigations* repeatedly emphasizes the importance of the "stream of life" which gives linguistic utterances their meaning (p. 261). The problem is that the topics of the later writings are still not the "meaning of life." This involves God-questions, and so philosophy is not completely brought around to those issues uppermost in Wittgenstein's life. Philosophy becomes for him the attempt to get rid of a particular kind of puzzlement, i.e., the puzzles of language. But on the other hand he said: "Philosophy ought really to be written as a *poetic composition*" (p. 291). On the one hand grammar is a mirror of reality, but on the other poetry shows us what is real. But if philosophy is a technique for achieving clarity, poetry lies at another extreme.

Next, philosophy becomes "a synopsis of trivialities" (p. 298). It is reduced to a matter of skill (p. 299). He offered a means to escape any need of theory; he did not offer us one (p. 301). In this way philosophy is driven further away from the concerns of life, rather than turning to deal with them. In a real sense, the door left open in the *Tractatus* is now closed. Philosophy becomes hardly at all aware of the mystical. The certainty sought by the *Tractatus* is achieved by abandoning systematic construction. Reality is not denied; it is there. But the techniques of philosophy are even further restricted from offering us direct attention. Russell's discovery of contradictions in Frege's logic had excited Wittgenstein. "He now wanted to declare such contradictions trivial" (p. 306).

In language we play games, and a careful consideration of the context can clear up puzzles and relieve mental cramps. Philosophy now provides a finality different from the *Tractatus*. But "just as speech is not essential in religion, so words cannot be essential to revealing what is true, or deep, in metaphysics" (p. 309). When philosophers confine themselves to philosophy as Wittgenstein comes to outline its work, they are even further from "reality" than they were with the assured connections of the *Tractatus*. Philosophy becomes a "simple" activity, but at the same time he reports that he spent much of his time meditating, praying, and reading the Bible (p. 318). The gulf between professional and personal life becomes ever wider as his "new approach to philosophical problems" develops.

"If there were theses in philosophy, they would have to be such that they do not give rise to disputes" (pp. 320-21). "As long as there is a possibility of having different opinions and disputing about a question, this indicates that things have not yet been expressed clearly enough. Once a perfectly clear formulation... has been reached, there can be no second thoughts or reluctance anymore" (pp. 320-21). Odd, the *Tractatus* had achieved finality by leaving the "mystical" outside. Then that which is outside philosophy's grasp becomes increasingly important, but "philosophy" shrinks in its scope. About the mystical, ethics, there can always be dispute. Has philosophy been sealed in the fly bottle—in the hope that it will be content with its games?

Grammar replaces theory in philosophy, so is it any wonder that Wittgenstein urged his students to avoid teaching philosophy. That could not be where his heart was. "Academic life was detestable" (p. 323). Of course, since it could not deal with what was—by his continued admission—most meaningful. Philosophy had tormented him, but now "the real discovery is the one that makes me capable of stopping doing philosophy when I want to—the one that gives philosophy peace, so that it is no longer tormented by questions which bring *itself* in question" (p. 325). Philosophy as a task of clarification has no end. Consider this statement against the life of a man whose whole existence was torment and involved the practice of rigorous ascetic discipline.

We know that he never ceased to call himself into question and that his life did not see problems vanish or even be much clarified. Philosophy was brought up against reality in the *Tractatus* but prevented from expressing it because logical structure did not permit propositions about the mystical. Now it is turned in upon itself and is able to reach "peace" only by restriction. Wittgenstein cannot have thought that all of importance was expressed in language games, although ordinary language does bring him closer. However, philosophy does not exhaust life's meaning. When ascetic practice strives for truth, philosophy becomes neutral.

Philosophy, like mathematics, becomes a series of techniques. Do we "answer" questions? It does not matter. What matters is that we see how arbitrary *any* answer would be (p. 331). This is now said by the man whose search drove him into battle, to the doorsteps of monasteries, to a hermit's isolation, to menial hospital work, to abandon wealth, and even to move away from a life of work with students. And yet with all this developing, philosophy in another aspect is modeled on Augustine's *Confessions* and becomes ritual purification and a quest for forgiveness, a strain never missing in Wittgenstein's life. But as he moved philosophy technically away from the center of meaning and concern in his life, so in his frequent moves he often left someone behind whom he loved (p. 361). For Wittgenstein *all* philosophy still "begins with a confession" (p. 366).

What gets in the way of understanding is one's pride. Thus "the edifice of your pride has to be dismantled. And this is very hard work" (p. 366). But contrast this approach to philosophy with that outlined above, one which is personally dispassionate and purely a matter of developed technique. The Socratic maxim returns: "If you are unwilling to know what you are, your writing is a form of deceit" (p. 367). Wittgenstein wrote out a personal confession and was going to read it to members of his family. He wrote: "Last year with God's help I pulled myself together and made a confession" (p. 372). But doing philosophy in no way needs "God's help." Self-purging and "descending into himself" is not necessary.

Wittgenstein sought "the transformation of his own despair into faith" (p. 376). But in philosophy he sought its transformation into a method that removes mental conflict. He speaks of his own "rotten nature," (p. 277) which evidences both the monk's sense of sin and the primary impulse to the religious life. He hated Braithwaite's "lack of seriousness" (p. 378); the monk lives under a weight of seriousness. But this "heaviness" is just what he purposes to lift from philosophy. He reflects on the need to lead a pure life. Can philosophy show him a way to clear up this perplexity? Personally he says: "God, if you do not help me, what can I do?" (p. 382). At the same time philosophical work is being removed from God and from need of help.

If wisdom and speculation are all we have, then "we are in a sort of hell where we can do nothing but dream, roofed in, as it were, and cut off from heaven" (p. 383). "And faith is faith in what is needed by my *heart*, my *soul*, not my speculative intelligence" (p. 383). Only love can believe in Jesus' resurrection. Philosophy does not bring one to it. Philosophical work is split off even further from that which occupies his life. "What combats doubt is, as it were, *redemption*" (p. 383). Philosophy is to rid you of doubts, but not of that kind. "First, you must be redeemed"(p. 384). Then everything will be different. Philosophy could relieve mental cramps. Wittgenstein could try to confess his sins, but this did not break into his loneliness.

The people Wittgenstein influenced most strongly did not enter academic life (p. 403). We can now understand that, since he was more aware than anyone of how far his conception of professional philosophy was drifting away from, or was cut off from (more drastically than in the *Tractatus*), all that absorbed him intently. Wittgenstein thought that, if he could overcome himself "then God would, as it were, come to him; he would then be saved" (p. 410). This is the mystic quest, the mystic belief, and its route is ascetic practice, not philosophical discussion of language games. Both enterprises are real; they are just unconnected, so that the practice of philosophy is of no advantage and may in fact work against the goal if it blocks ascetic discipline.

Monk notes: "In the context of his search for redemption through the dismantling of his pride, Wittgenstein's philosophical work occupies a curiously ambivalent place" (p. 413). It was the greatest source of his pride. Yet, as he "clips philosophy's wings," lessens its scope and goals, has pride in its accomplishments (such as the *Tractatus*) diminishes too, since philosophy's work is no longer monumental. Are the two connected? Does the relegation of philosophy to the role of clarifying, to the examination of language games, at the same time make it impossible to be "proud" of one's work? If so, those following Wittgenstein's lead will dismantle their pride with his. But for him this becomes a means to redemption too, which it is difficult to grasp.

"It is important to Wittgenstein's conception of his philosophical method that there could be no differences of opinion..." (p. 419). This could only come about, he thought, because words were being used in a different way. "It could only be a question of giving meaning to words" (p. 419). "The whole point is that I must not have an opinion" (p. 420).

There should not be substantive differences of opinion; yet a storm rages in his own life between opinions he can neither reconcile nor dispel. "Philosophy" cannot be turned to help him in this task. Contradictions abound in his life; this he would not deny, but they are not in philosophy. "A contradiction cannot lead me astray because it leads nowhere at all" (p. 421).

Philosophy did not cause his own problems to disappear. As late as 1942 he wrote: "I no longer feel any hope for the future of my life" (p. 442). "The main thing is still loneliness" (p. 442). "I have suffered so much, but I am apparently incapable of *learning* from my life. I still suffer *just* as I did many years ago. I have not become any stronger or wiser" (p. 443). Hearing this and recognizing both Wittgenstein's intellect and his assignment of philosophy to a lesser role, one thinks of Kierkegaard's comment: it was intellect that had to be opposed, and perhaps, Kierkegaard said, that is why he was given such an strong intellect. Wittgenstein's aim in philosophy was "to give an expression such form that certain disquietudes disappear" (p. 446). But this did not happen in his life.

"An honest religious thinker is like a tightrope walker" (p. 464). "I am not a religious man but I cannot help seeing every problem from a religious point of view," he reports (p. 464). Wisdom is gray. Life on the other hand and religion are full of color. "The passion of religious faith is the only thing capable of overcoming the deadness of theory," Monk comments (p. 490). His view of philosophy's task was internally colorless. One only needed to be competent. In love, although he felt a deep need for it, he often felt himself incapable, frightened. But love cannot be taken; "it has to be bestowed as a gift" (p. 492). However, Monk concludes, that was never Wittgenstein's good fortune.

The aim of his philosophical method was to change the aspect under which certain things are seen. "What I do is suggest, or even invent, other ways of looking at it" (p. 502). We are now familiar with this view of philosophy, but it grows paradoxical when seen in relation to the anxieties of his life and perplexing when placed against his negative views about philosophy as a profession. Philosophy "leaves everything as it is." That remark of Wittgenstein is often repeated. But when he speaks of his melancholy and says he cannot see how he will ever be freed from guilt (p. 534), we have the odd contrast of quietude in philosophy and an anguished desire for personal change. However, he enforced a strict separation of philosophy from religion and practice.

"The *words* you utter or what you think as you utter them are not what matters, so much as the difference they make at various points in your life." Wittgenstein concludes: *"Practice* gives the words their sense" (p. 573). Here is the contrast: philosophy is a self-contained activity clarifying language structure and leaving all as it was. This is contrasted with the demand that words have meaning only if embodied in life, in practice, in action. Of course, ordinary language gives philosophy a context, but the "primitive" uses of language are still detached from changed lives. He wanted to complete the *Investigations* before his death. But something else was more important: his reconciliation with God, Monk concludes (p. 573).

We reach the end of doubt only in practice. "You must look at the practice of languages," Wittgenstein advises (p. 579). That takes philosophy a step toward the seriousness of embodiment in action. But Wittgenstein struggled with much more than language. He lived "a devoutly religious life," Monk believes (p. 580). But this was in the sense of a state of ethical seriousness and ascetic practice, more than as the practice of clarifying language. In fact, Wittgenstein thought one could not tell what someone believed by examining his words, only by his life in action. "In the beginning was the deed," he quotes Goethe. So much more than language, or even philosophy as he came to practice it, Wittgenstein's "quest for the holy grail" was the quest for practice, for the ascetically stringent life.

5 THE MYSTICAL WITHIN LANGUAGE

In the *Philosophical Grammar* Wittgenstein has told us that "what belongs to grammar are all the conditions (the method) necessary for comparing the proposition with reality"[1] (p. 106). The mystical lay outside this. Grammar kept language clear and pure. Now, however, we have reason to doubt that. As Wittgenstein turned from the clear structure of propositions in the *Tractatus*, did he begin to find in language structure, now ordinary languages not that of the *Tractatus*, some of the mystical he had recognized and valued but placed outside the definitive structure of logical prepositions?

If the two merge, if grammar alone does not tell us how to compare language with reality, understanding will become less clear, less definitive, and the mystical breaks over the barriers holding it back from language. "Reality" too may prove more illusive in our attempted comparison, since we counted on the clarity of grammar to make the comparison with reality possible. If the mystical "invades" language, the whole project of finality is in jeopardy. Philosophy does not now create new, ideal languages but only clarifies the uses of our language, the existing language. Clarity will be more difficult, if not ultimately impossible in crucial cases, if the structure of language itself allows mysticism within.

Language no longer simply represents the world. Linguistic expressions have a wide variety of functions. Logic is now concerned with *our* language, but, if so, can it be purged of unclarities? If the essence of language was a picture of the world, "philosophy as the custodian of grammar could in fact grasp the essence of the world" (p. 109). The nonsensical combination of signs was excluded in order to make this possible. But as Wittgenstein turns to ordinary language and practice, is the rigid line of distinction broken down, in spite of his new

---

[1] As quoted in J.C. Nyiri, ed., *Austrian Philosophy: Studies and Texts*, Philosophia Verlag, Munich, 1981.

desire to achieve a sense of finality in the analysis of language games, the finality of the *Tractatus* having proved artificial? The world of the *Tractatus* was an immobile logical paradise.

Now we must turn to the "labyrinth of paths" in language. Context gives meaning its importance. The activity of philosophy is learned through concrete examples. "It is precisely to these infinitely complex relations that one must turn in order to solve the philosophical problems that disturb us" (p. 121). To imagine language now means to imagine a form of life, but it is clear that in Wittgenstein's life the mystical played an immense part, which the *Tractatus* had once locked outside. If philosophical perplexity is a mental cramp that can be analyzed in language so that we can rid ourselves of perplexity, that again requires finality in analysis. But this cannot be, if the form of life which language images involves the mystical.

There may be rules governing the use of expressions which we can explore, but what if the content of the experience embodied does itself not entirely conform to rules? Why does language become so confused in the first place so that it gives us mental cramps and requires analysis? Could it be that the puzzles will only disappear intellectually (perhaps) but that its source in the life of the individual will not be eradicated? This seems to have been Wittgenstein's experience in his own restlessness with philosophy in comparison with his personal struggles. He developed a method in philosophy for clearing up puzzles in language, but it did not seem to touch his life. Wittgenstein does not explore the social, the personal, the material source of speech.

If philosophical problems did resemble a "sickness" and if the new method dissolves the perplexity in language, with Wittgenstein's increasing stress on the practical embodiment of thought in action, we must look to the person in philosophy and see the change in the person's life, according to Wittgenstein's own account. This is why his method has been compared to psychoanalysis, a suggestion which he did not accept. But the important difference is that Freud is the ultimate rationalist and is sure the touch of reasonable words will expose and cure the tortured emotion. Wittgenstein, on the other hand, has a strong sense of the mystical so that, if language embodies that aspect of life, the clarity so carefully preserved in the *Tractatus* is invaded.

Kierkegaard, whom Wittgenstein read, spoke of "The Sickness Unto Death" which could not be dispelled although it could be dealt with. If philosophy's "sickness," which Wittgenstein proposes a method to cure, comes close to Kierkegaard's ultimate complexities as language expresses them, then the perplexities of language even if removed leave the life beneath, their source, still in anguish. "Alienation," Kierkegaard's central concept, may be formed in the self and simply manifest itself linguistically. Freud can hope to remove the source by "pure reason," by analysis, but Wittgenstein knows the deep effects of the mystical in the person. Thus, Wittgenstein does not want philosophy divorced from the actual sources of language in our lives. But this allows the mystical "inside" language, and it left Wittgenstein no rest in his own life as a philosopher.

To relieve our mental cramp, to resolve the puzzle, we must ask why it would occur to Wittgenstein to turn from logical structure in seeking to replace philosophy's task which was lost after the *Tractatus*. Logical, propositional structure had never been "all." Reality and the mystical were beyond and were referred to. When the finality/certainty of this project proved impossible, "language" seems a poor substitute and an unlikely candidate for releasing the tension which was built up by "locking outside" the logical structure that which was so important to Wittgenstein. "Language," of course, now means "ordinary" language, not the propositional construction offered in the *Tractatus*.

A. Jewish Mysticism

Since it was "the mystical," the unspeakable outside propositional structure which interested Wittgenstein in the *Tractatus* and came to occupy his biography even more as time went on, let us examine some notions of mysticism and their accounts of its relation to language to see if this offers us any clue. Gershom Scholem's *Major Trends in Jewish Mysticism*[2] is a good start. Wittgenstein is Christian by family conversion, but Jewish and Christian mysticism by his time had many common threads, plus the fact that we are not looking for actual historical influence but merely to see if another treatment of the "mystical" might be illuminating. Since, as we will argue, had it not been for the mystical left outside the *Tractatus*, Wittgenstein's views might not have changed to take the form they did.

Given the Enlightenment, Modern, and Rationalist trends, Jews themselves were unsympathetic, even repelled, by the Kabbalah and Hasidism. It seemed to scholars darkly to stand in their path (p. 1), which makes it all the more unusual (since the same is true for Christians of the day) that Wittgenstein would tie mysticism as he does

---

[2] Schockem Books, New York, 1941.

into a "logico-philosophicus" treatise. It is important to note that it is not Wittgenstein's "rationalism" that forces him to place mysticism in the "unspeakable" realm. "Adequate description" has always been a great riddle for the mystics themselves. Since the experience is "of a highly contradictory and even paradoxical nature," (p. 2) it blocks its own expression.

Where God is concerned, the mystics agree that "the help of words," naming in a metaphorical sense, "are not real names at all" (p. 12) and thus are outside the logical structure. But it is also true that no single interpretation of the Torah is capable of taking in its meaning (p. 14), so that the observant Jew does not need to be "mystical" to see the limitation of propositional language. Since mystical knowledge is related to a sphere "where speech and expression are excluded," (p. 13) how is lingual expression possible? The mystic's feelings cannot be expressed adequately. Yet they glory in them (their expressions) as Wittgenstein came to do too. But a contradiction emerges: first, a striking restraint in referring to their experience, and then "their metaphysically positive attitude towards language as God's own instrument" (p. 13).

Here is one key in the transition to the *Investigations*. The *Tractatus* is "restrained," to say the least, in what is said about the mystical (or what can not be said); the *Investigations* acts as if language were "God's own instrument," else why should it be given such exhaulted attention? The autobiographies of the mystics are the key to their literature; it is Wittgenstein's biography which opens his work to a wider setting. However, the Kabbalists' personalities do not intrude into their objective descriptions, just as Wittgenstein's is absent in the *Tractatus* but is emerging in the *Investigations*. All Kabbalists agree in regarding language a something more precious than an "inadequate instrument for contact between human beings" (p. 17).

The "mystical" once excluded from logical propositions now returns in the high value set on the insightfulness of "ordinary language." The Kabbalist sees in speech "a key to the deepest secrets of the Creator and his Creation" (p. 18). (Recall: we are not saying that Wittgenstein put it in these terms). But "Kabbalah" literally means "tradition," and it is a new tradition Wittgenstein sought to inaugurate, that concept so important to both Jews and Roman Catholics. But because the knowledge gained was "secret," it is difficult to impart. And Wittgenstein exhibits all the characteristics of a master imparting esoteric teachings to the uninitiated. The Kabbalists used ordinary terms, but their "magic hand" opened up hidden sources of meaning (p. 24).

Does "ordinary language" serve for Wittgenstein as a set of symbols which open "deeper" meaning? For the Kabbalist, symbols through their own existence makes "another reality transparent which cannot appear in any other form" (p. 27). "The Jewish mystic lives and acts in a perpetual rebellion against a world with which he strives with all his zeal to be at peace" (p. 34). Is this not clear in Wittgenstein's biography, Cambridge vs. a Norwegian hut, Viennese wealth vs. a monk's ascetic life? For the Kabbalist, "his mystic ascent is always preceded by ascetic practices" (p. 45). What else would drive a wealthy aristocrat to poverty and simplistic isolation? For the Kabbalist, "there is almost no love of God," (vs. much for Christian mysticism) and love is strangely missing for Wittgenstein, agonizingly so.

Did Wittgenstein seek in a sense to open a "Messianic Age" for philosophy? "That which belongs to the domain of secret lore shall become universal knowledge in the Messianic age," Scholem reports (p. 72). Wittgenstein's instructions in philosophy had all the trappings of dispensing "secret lore," yet they were intended to inaugurate a new age. "Messianism" is a common phenomenon in both Christianity and Judaism. Is there a parallel with the Talmudic scholar too, about which Scholem says: "Nowhere else was so much importance assigned to learning, so much zeal developed in the pursuit of study" (p. 80). Certainly Wittgenstein did not take teaching, or his students, casually. Philosophy as an ascetic practice? Three things go to make up the Hasid: ascetic renunciation of the things of the world; complete serenity of mind; and "an altruism grounded in principle and driven to extremes" (p. 92).

Wittgenstein's biography exhibits all three, except for the personal tragedy that he strove for serenity of mind and never attained it. It is said that "the ascetic turn of mind is a corollary of a darkly pessimistic attitude toward life," (p. 92) which Wittgenstein had in plenty but which unfortunately was never matched by serenity of mind. Would Wittgenstein have had to abandon his rationalism, his logic, his mathematics, had he sought to follow the mystic tradition? No, that relieves the central paradox too easily. "This affinity of the mystic with the great rationalist has its astounding parallel" (p. 126). He can be, he was, both.

After the *Tractatus* was Wittgenstein torn over whether he should write and publish philosophy? One of the Kabbalists expressed it: "I want to write it down and I am not allowed to do it; I do not want to write it down and cannot entirely desist," (p. 127) as Wittgenstein's literary executors know. Following philosophy is a harsh life, as Wittgenstein presented it, but the Kabbalists thought that "the purpose of this discipline...is to stimulate...a new state of consciousness" (p. 133). The Kabbalist "lays great emphasis on the newness and singularity of his prophecy" (p.138). And there is evidence that Wittgenstein's appearances in Cambridge were treated after the mode of the prophet.

The Zohar assumes that "the process of life in God can be construed as the unfolding of the elements of speech" (p. 216). So that, probably unknown to Wittgenstein, the concentration on language is an access to the life of God which was closed off in the *Tractatus*. These "games," then, are all important to our greater understanding. Such knowledge as we gain "cannot be communicated directly but may be expressed only through symbol and metaphor"[3] (p. 4). And there is a "clear tendency toward asceticism as a way of preparing for the reception of the mystical tradition" (p. 11). The concept of the mysticism of language means that "the speech of men is connected to divine speech and all language..." (p. 46). Mysteries are disclosed that had previously been hidden.

Perle Epstein tells us that "Jews continued to display a penchant for teacher worship that is still evident today"[4] (p. xvi). Certainly Wittgenstein followers have tended to form a cult. Yet the sage must be perfectly stable, perfectly ethical (p. 3), and the struggle to achieve this balance is clear in Wittgenstein's life. But first intellectual confusion must be cleared away (p. 3), again a constant goal for Wittgenstein. And if "there cannot be any progress on the spiritual path without concomitant physical behavior," (p. 7) Wittgenstein's constant ascetic discipline qualifies him for that search. "The ascetic mode of life is essential to their moral survival" (p. 9). "The function of understanding was to provide him with a weapon against worldliness" (p. 16).

The theme: "For one can arrive at the limit of a person's knowledge, but not at the limit of his thought" (p. 43). In this vein we can regard the *Tractatus* as the limit of his "knowledge" and the intense struggle after that as pressing the limits of thought. "The journey's end is a place where human speech cannot follow" (p. 51); rigorous ascetic practice is needed to take us beyond that point. Was Wittgenstein essentially on a

---

[3] G. Scholan. *Kabbalah*, New American Library, New York, 1978.
[4] *Kabbalah*. Shambhala, Boston, 1978.

"spiritual journey"? "Abraham's arduous spiritual pilgrimage, detailed in the esoteric tales of his wanderings... ended when he reached the level of illumination called *Wisdom*" (p. 62).

The *Zohar* emphasizes the unity of word, thought, and energy (p. 64). Certainly Wittgenstein's biography reflects this. More important perhaps: "For the Jewish mystic, the Hebrew language has always corresponded physically to the thing it designated. Merely writing a Hebrew letter could produce a unifying effect on the mind and body, putting one in touch with the 'higher' world" (p. 73). And note this parallel: "By taking the word inside out of itself, playfully shaking it loose from its denotative meaning, and melting it down as he led his rapt disciples from rational discourse to the realm of pure, non-verbal perception" [showing], the master "...directed the novice out of the circular and restricting round of thought" (pp. 73-74). Does this not describe Wittgenstein's teaching too?

In his late work Wittgenstein comes to reflect on the beginning of speech. And introspection is a Kabbalist mode: "Look into yourself and you will come to find the beginning of thought," (p. 84) although Wittgenstein takes his lead from Augustine's *Confessions*. But "meditating on words evokes the true, formless meaning of their hidden nature" (p. 105). Their puzzles are resolved. The Hasid's role in life "consisted in stripping away illusion," (p. 121) and Wittgenstein certainly saw himself in this light too. But "along this path lay the danger of insanity," (p. 143) with which Wittgenstein struggled constantly. "No real teacher of the Kabbalah will advertise" (p. 163). Wittgenstein did everything to keep followers away.

B. CHRISTIAN MYSTICISM

Although there are certain themes in Jewish mysticism which may illuminate Wittgenstein's life and work, in fact in his life he paid more attention to Christianity. If we are to consider language and the mystic, no Christian writer could be a better source than Dionysius the Areopagite. *On the Divine Names*, and *The Mystical Theology*[5] take up the issue of intelligible speech (or its possibility) about God. We see the theme when he states: "I will proceed, so far as in me lies, to an exposition of the Divine Names" (p. 51). Although he does not separate the sayable from the unsayable as strictly as Wittgenstein does, he indicates that clear exposition is an impossibility.

---

[5] Trans. C.E. Rolt, SPCK Press, London, 1934.

Truth can only be declared "in a manner surpassing speech and knowledge," (p. 51) which exceeds the exercise of discourse or intuitive reason. We cannot speak or form any conception of God, we are told, and Wittgenstein's view is similar. God surpasses the apprehension of thought, and beyond utterance it surpasses the reach of words (p. 53). As Wittgenstein warns his readers in the *Tractatus*, so Dionysius says, "do not seek with impotent presumption the Mystery" (p. 54). "But at present we employ (so far as in us lies), appropriate symbols for things Divine" (p. 58). But Wittgenstein has only logical propositions. He cannot use symbols and so stops instead of going ahead to attempt description. But Dionysius moves to paradox: "The sacred Writers celebrate it by ever Name while yet they call it nameless" (p. 61).

While Wittgenstein backs away in the *Tractatus*, Dionysius presses on: "such knowledge of Divine truth as is possible must not be disregarded" (p. 85). For him the separation is not absolute; it may be bridged but not completely or finally. Wittgenstein sought finality in the *Tractatus* which excluded such a compromise with mysticism. What he calls "negative knowledge" (we express in a transcendent manner by negative images) (p. 90) opens an avenue for Dionysius, but Wittgenstein can accept only direct attribution. This is reversed for Dionysius, principally because Non-Existence can be ascribed to God. Yet "God" is difficult to express, because "God is not Existent in any ordinary sense but in a simple and indefinable manner embracing and anticipating all existence in Himself" (p. 135). On the other hand, Wittgenstein demands clear definition.

Where Dionysius says: "Hence all attributes may be affirmed at once of Him, and yet He is No Thing," (p. 140) we face a situation difficult for a logician to express. And so it is left inexpressible. Since God "even transcends all Reason, Intelligence, and Wisdom," (p. 146) the human intellect is communing with things that exceed its intellectual nature. Wittgenstein recommends silence and Dionysius does too, but in a different way. The mysteries of truth "lie hidden in the dazzling obscurity of the secret Silence" (p. 191). The true initiate plunges into "the Darkness of Unknowing" (p. 194). But Wittgenstein holds back from such a plunge, recognizing the boundary all the while.

Such darkness produces "absolute dumbness of both speech and thought" (p. 198). Wittgenstein says the same in milder terms while warning us not to trespass by using propositions. It is helpful to see, thus, how similar in situation Wittgenstein and the mystical tradition are. Wittgenstein does not move forward in the *Tractatus* to say what he can, as they do, but rather the opposite. Yet his own approach takes place as his life proceeds by using other means and instruments than propositions. "Showing" is important, as is embodiment in deed. What cannot be talked about directly still shows itself in other ways, and we must deal with it.

The *Cloud of Unknowing* is written by an anonymous author,[6] but the expression might have suited Wittgenstein well. The mind becomes blank before what it cannot assimilate. It enters a cloud of unknowing. In dealing with this, suffering is involved (as Wittgenstein knows). One feels desolation and dismay. This leads to a crisis hour, we are told. And love is the guide, not thought. However, much as Wittgenstein needed love, he seemed unable to draw much from it, as the mystic must when thought cannot move further. We are told that the sinner will find such a life of contemplation difficult, and Wittgenstein never ceased to be aware of that block. There is a necessary stage in any progress, the solitary. That Wittgenstein was aware of and practiced, although not consistently.

The darkness and the cloud "remain between you and God" (p. 53). The mystic passes through with humble love, which Wittgenstein knew he could not do. God cannot be comprehended by the intellect but by love. All rational beings possess two faculties: "the power of knowing and the power of loving" (p. 55). Wittgenstein had the first in superabundance; he agonized greatly over the second, wanted it, but never seemed able to possess it. The mystic is also advised to "pay attention to this marvelous work of grace within your soul," (p. 57) something Wittgenstein needed but evidently never received. The mystic is warned not to attempt "to achieve this experience intellectually" (p. 58). Wittgenstein knows that to be impossible but could never fully stop trying.

Wittgenstein struggled in his life with the mystics' motto: "By love he can be caught and held, but by thinking never" (p. 60). He knew it was impossible for him to stop thinking, but he knew its sad effect upon love too. "Reason becomes evil when pride inflates it," (p. 63) and Wittgenstein struggled under "the duty of genius," as Ray Monk puts it. In later years, Wittgenstein could just as well have ended the *Tractatus* with the mystics theme: "Love may reach up to God himself even in this life—but not knowledge" (p. 63). The *Tractatus* in that sense concludes on a negative note, one which has been put more positively by others.

---

[6] Trans. Clifton Walters, Penguin Books, Middlesex, England, 1961.

However, he did follow the advice for humility: "Strain every nerve in every possible way to know and experience yourself as you really are" (p. 71).

However, the mystic does caution us: "The other... the urgent movement of love—is wholly God's work" (p. 86). Being unable to believe in God, as Wittgenstein said, he was blocked to go beyond the cloud of unknowing; love cannot be had by trying. It is a gift and one Wittgenstein either never received or at least did all too seldom. Of course, "whomever would work at becoming a contemplative must first cleanse his conscience," (p. 88) and we know Wittgenstein struggled with that constantly, although never to his satisfaction. "Everybody finds this work extremely hard," (p. 88) we are told, and Wittgenstein certainly did. However, the object is never attained by study, "but only by grace" (p. 99). This he never experienced.

As genius must, Wittgenstein had an intense awareness of his own existence. And it was not comforting. The mystic writer asks: "You will ask me next how to destroy this stark awareness or your own existence" (p. 103). But this stark awareness cannot possibly be destroyed "without God's very special and freely given grace" (p. 103). We know that Wittgenstein lived with thoughts of suicide at times, and it is also very clear that he did not experience God's "grace." In fact, he does not seem to have known what it meant, in spite of his interest in Christianity. He was, then, locked within himself, anxious for release from that burden, but never released from the fly bottle, because intellect could not be the means.

C. The Platonist's Concept of Language: a Suggestion

If what is mystical can appear within language and not be held outside as the *Tractatus* wanted to do, it raises for us the question of language and its function, which can never be taken for granted. Wittgenstein was not himself a trained linguist, and there is such a field that studies all the known languages of the world and their structures. Within philosophy proper, we know there have been and are other views about the function of language besides Wittgenstein's. Unless we accept the Positivists, who reject all of an earlier date and expect to achieve unanimity of theory now, we must always stay ready to examine other concepts of language, as Wittgenstein in fact did. Let us offer him a post-mortem alternative.

Plato, for instance, thought that ordinary language was full of vagueness and unexamined definitions of crucial terms, and so it could not be clarifying or helpful in itself. True, his dialogues, which develop and clarify meanings, are somewhat similar to Wittgenstein's discourses, except that Plato never expected finality. The main difficulty stems from the fact that, for Plato, the most important terms, e.g. "good," "justice," "love," are subject to the greatest variety of definitions. His confidence: our disagreements over these may be brought to light with benefit. Yet, only insignificant terms can be finally settled as to meaning.

Ordinary speech as we hear it in the market place, in bars, is full of vulgarity and crudeness and imprecision and unexamined bias. It is the philosopher's task to provide a clarity about crucial terms which everyday language itself does not provide. Ordinary discourse tends to use terms without definitions, which the philosopher supplies, not the speakers or raw language itself. Is, then, only the rare utterance profound, not the many ordinary ones? We cannot dismiss the possibility that enlightenment comes from esoteric language more than from ordinary language.

Reality was not locked within language for Wittgenstein. The mystical remains outside and "reality" must too, since only a comparison to reality makes the truth of propositions evident. In the method of philosophy in the *Investigations* and later, all is still not brought within language, although language may provide the key to its own clarification if properly approached. But if Wittgenstein himself had at least two views of the function of language and rejected final philosophical system building, the nature and function of language in philosophy will always remain an open question—for him and for us.

(1) The Contemporary Use of Negative Theology[7]

Theology is out of fashion in many philosophical circles today, but the negative method which it made famous is very much in use. Linguistic analysis, which might be supposed to be the group most opposed to any theological device, may be said to use "the negative method" whenever the ontological status of language is concerned. Medieval theologians, borrowing from Platonists and from Dionysius the Areopagite, developed this as a way of making it possible for them to talk about the nature of God. God was an object of such immensity that their minds could not approach divinity directly, as Wittgenstein pointed out. They needed a method of indirection. Many of those who follow the

---

[7] This section is adapted from an article in *The Journal of Philosophy*, Vol. LI, No. 25, Dec. 9, 1954, pp. 823-830.

analytic school deny the possibility of dealing with ontological questions such as God. But according to the thesis developed here, by reappraising Wittgenstein's life and work the analysis of language cannot avoid questions of ontology or metaphysics. In that sense, Wittgenstein too was involved in negative ontology, since he gave answers to ontological issues by indirection, as medieval theologians did. No discussion of language can avoid doing so, since the very nature and status of language necessarily leads immediately to the heart of metaphysics. It cannot be locked outside, as Wittgenstein first hoped to do.

If we apply the negative method, the view of the ontological status of language which emerges is about as follows: in analyzing language and treating it as an object of study of the first order, sentences have been reified into things and treated in a manner which grants language a kind of reality and independent status of its own. When language is treated as an object capable of study in isolation, its derived and secondary status is implicitly denied. We are left in the position of asserting by indirection that language has an ontological status of the first order and is, therefore, capable of being studied without reference to anything other than itself, although Wittgenstein knew that there were other important considerations.

A careful study of the Platonic tradition yields a very different concept of the ontological status and function of language, one which Wittgenstein might find congenial, had circumstances been different. On this view, words are an indispensable tool in the knowing process. They have a natural relation to things in the world and to the objects of knowledge, such that sentences are, at times, capable of expressing the structure of nature. Yet, in spite of this valuable and natural function, language has a dependent and derived existence, since things of the world would still exist if knowledge should disappear, while neither language nor knowledge could exist alone, if the objects to which language refers should cease to exist.

Therefore, since language depends on something other than itself for its meaning, it cannot be studied on its own or in isolation; propositions and words must be treated as merely the signs of things other than themselves. If it is to be helpful to us in dealing with philosophical problems, the study of language must lead finally to a study of the nature of these things whose structure language merely reflects. Since the function of language is to illustrate the structure of things, a study of language takes us, through the structure of language, back to a study of the basic structure of the world.

(2) The Ontological Status of Language Structure

If the Platonists view of the status of language is correct, why have we thought that we could study language structure without reference to anything else? Plato suggests an answer when he says, "wisdom is the only science which is the science of itself as well as of the other sciences."[8] This being true, a language which expresses knowledge can study itself as well as other things. Dwelling on this unique self-reflective capacity, we tend to forget that, in spite of its special adaptability for self-study, the central function of language is to direct our attention to things other than itself. Language can become egocentric, stressing its own self-analysis, forgetting its derived and dependent status. If so, what we sometimes fail to see is that ultimately we must study the structure of the world, and at least momentarily, we must forget language structure if we want to be philosophically fruitful.

"Then we agree that words are signs?"[9]—Augustine asks. Since signs in turn refer to thought and thought to things, this means that language is most often a sign of something other than itself and should be an object of study only incidentally. Knowledge exists only because "objects" have been apprehended, and language is meaningful only because of the prior existence of knowledge. Therefore, "words exist in order that they may be used, and in addition we use them in order to teach" (p. 37). We use words in teaching only in order to direct the attention of others toward the knowledge which we have previously apprehended. But the teacher knows that, ultimately, the student must learn for himself/herself.

As Augustine says, cognition is the aim of language and must be considered superior to the sign "for the sole reason that it is proved conclusively that the sign exists because of the cognition and not the cognition because of the sign" (p. 36). Had nothing been apprehended by the mind, words would not exist or have a function to perform. If the status of language is that of a sign which has come into existence in order that we may teach, i.e., directing another person's attention by manipulating propositions, Augustine's admonition is understandable: "I have warned you that we should not attribute more to words than is proper" (p. 55).

"What does it seem to you that we wish to accomplish when we speak?" (p. 3), Augustine asks, and the Platonist's answer is that we wish

---

[8] Plato, *Charmides*, 166, trans. by Jowett, Vol. I, p. 17, New York, 1937.
[9] Augustine, *Concerning the Teacher*, p. 6, trans. by Leckie, Appleton-Century, New York, 1938.

to use language as a tool whereby we can, hopefully, cause the real object of knowledge to be cognized. What exactly, then, is the power of language? "To give them as much credit as possible, words possess only sufficient efficacy to remind us in order that we may seek things, but not to exhibit the things so that we may know them" (p. 46). Propositions in themselves are by nature weak, but they are, fortunately, just strong enough, sometimes at least, to stimulate the mind and to point out the direction to the objects of knowledge. Language, and the interest in its structure, must not be allowed to become so rigid or to absorb so much of our attention that reality cannot be seen "peering through" the words, since language was originally designed as a means to summon our attention to cognize objects.

(3) What Can We Learn From a Study of Language?

Since it does not have an end in itself, language is designed to reflect the structure of the objects which it discusses. Therefore, it would seem that some knowledge of structures and relations in the world might be gained from a study of the structure of language. This is true, but the fine line which needs to be drawn here is that language will not yield this knowledge if it is cut off to be dissected in isolation. In this case structure will be learned, but it will be artificial and slightly distorted and will resemble a game.

Language, unless it leads us to study natural structures themselves, can be the worst of all deceivers, since it has enough similarity (like a picture) to the structure of the world to give one who studies it a good imitation of real knowledge. "Now what is this thing, of which the Sophist himself has knowledge and gives knowledge to his pupil?"[10] We have the right to ask this Socratic question. If the answer is, that we are to gain knowledge only of how language is put together, its grammar, then we had better be sure that nothing more is claimed. But if we think that the analysis of language will in itself teach us something about the world, about reality, then we should be clear about the ontological relationship involved between language and its object.

"The knowledge of names is a great part of knowledge,"[11] but we ought not go any further without establishing just what part of knowledge the knowledge of names is and what other possible kinds of knowledge there may be. Otherwise, like Socrates in the *Cratylus*, we may fool ourselves into thinking that acquiring a little more knowledge

---

[10] Plato, *Protagoras*, 312e, Loeb Library trans., p. 105, London, 1952.
[11] Plato, *Cratylus*, 383, trans. by Jowett, Vol. I, p. 173.

of names would teach us all that we need to know. If we first establish the relation of language to knowledge, we will know what to expect and what not to expect from a study of propositional structure. If it is true, as Socrates goes on to suggest, that some things may come to be known without the mediation of language (438), and that some notions are grasped by the mind itself directly,[12] it is certain that language is neither the whole nor the sole approach to knowledge.

Language study, therefore, may in fact lead to knowledge, but it is not identical with knowledge nor the only possible object of philosophical study. "Most people are ignorant of the fact that they do not know the nature of things,"[13] Plato tells us, and this makes it all the easier to confuse some people into thinking that language is the thing which they most want to know and that it is to be identified with knowledge itself. They may be like the people Plato describes in the *Republic*, seated within the cave watching the procession of shadows, "if they could talk to one another, would they not suppose that their words referred only to those passing shadows which they saw?"[14] (514). And so explorers of language structure speaking to one another might suppose that their words referred only to the structure of language immediately before them. Whereas, once the relation of words to knowledge is recognized, language can be understood to be a shadow of something more significant, namely, the structure of the world itself.

Once we understand the relation of language to knowledge, we realize that "the knowledge itself which results from the sign should be considered superior to the sign."[15] That is, not only is the knowledge of language structure merely a part of knowledge, actually it is inferior to a knowledge of the objects of language themselves. Augustine concludes, "I am satisfied that it has been shown that the cognition of the thing which a sign signifies is more powerful than the sign itself..." (p. 39). And more: "the sign is learned after the thing is cognized is rather more the case than that the thing itself is learned after the sign is given" (p. 44).

Not only is the knowledge of language less powerful than the knowledge of objects themselves, but the fact is that we could not even learn the meaning of words if it were not that we had first cognized the objects to which the words referred. When language is studied in itself,

---

[12] Plato, *Theatetus*, 186a, Loeb Library trans., p. 163, London, 1912.
[13] Plato, *Phaedrus*, 237c, Loeb Library trans., p. 445, London, 1914.
[14] Plato, *Republic*, trans. by Cornford, p. 228, Oxford, New York, 1947.
[15] Augustine, op. cit., p. 36.

then, we may forget that in order to be significant at all words need to be preceded by a cognition of the structure of some object. Signs, therefore, cannot really teach us anything, since in order for the word to have meaning in the first place, the object to which it refers had to be cognized before the word could be attached.

We learn nothing unless we also see what the word mentions. "If he does learn, he learns by means of the things themselves and from his own senses, but not through the articulated words. For the same words are heard by the man who sees and by the man who does not see" (p. 49). Anselm agrees with Augustine here: "An object can hardly or ever be cognized according to the word alone."[16] Language may be the necessary, but it certainly is not the sufficient condition for knowledge. "Understanding an object," Anselm tells us, "is comprehending in knowledge its real existence" (p. 165). Examining language structure may aid us in this task, but in itself it can never do the job for us. For the completion of this process, for knowledge to be attained, the mind itself must be prepared, since its grasp of the object is the final test. "Little or nothing is the outer mirror," Bonaventura reminds us, "unless the mirror of the mind be clear and polished."[17] It must be ready to receive the information which language conveys to it. Oddly enough, Wittgenstein often said something quite like that.

The question of how knowledge, once contained in the mind and gained by means of language, is related to its object may for the Platonist be expressed by the following question: "Do you agree with him [Protagoras], or would you say that things have a permanent essence of their own?" (*Cratylus*, 386). If your answer is that things do have an independent existence and do not change as our opinion of then changes, then you believe that knowledge as it lies in the mind is merely a reflection of the structure of objects whose existence is independent from the mind. The business of knowledge is to reflect the structures which it observes. They (things) must be supposed to have their own proper and permanent essence; they are not dependent solely on their relation to us or even influenced by us, fluctuating according to our fancy. But they are independent and maintain to their own essence the relation prescribed by nature (*Cratylus*, 386).

---

[16] Anselm, *Appendix in Behalf of the Foll*, p. 149, trans. by Deane, Open Court, Chicago, 1939.

[17] Bonaventura, *The Mind's Road to God*, p. 5, trans. by Boas, Liberal Arts Press, New York, 1953.

Knowledge is, then, not free to take any course it wants, nor can language be designed in any fashion which pleases us, played like a game with conventional rules. Knowledge of our language must (or rather, should) observe the independent structure of things and adapt itself so as to reflect the object apprehended as faithfully as possible. "Then a name is an instrument of teaching and of distinguishing natures" (388). What should follow from this is that "he who knows names knows also the things which are expressed by them" (435).

The rules of language are not entirely of our own making; they should try to follow the tune which nature calls. "If a speech is to be good, must not the mind of the speaker know the truth about the matters of which he speaks?" (*Phaedrus*, 259e). If the mind knows the truth about its objects, speech cannot be allowed to go its own way; it must be marshaled to parallel the truth which the mind wants to express. Language, if it is to be useful, ought not to be allowed to "become its own boss." If language is ever thought to be an end in itself, we must again ask the question: "When a man knows, must there not be something that he knows?" (*Republic*, 476) This should redirect our attention away from language to knowledge and thence to the objects of knowledge themselves. "We have then: first, a name; second, a description; third, an image; and fourth, a knowledge of the object. And we must put as a fifth entity the actual object of knowledge which is the true reality"[18] (*Epistle VII*, 341d).

"Or does anyone, do you think, understand the name of anything when he does not know what the thing is?" (*Theatetus*, 147b). And to this question our answer must be "no." "If a man says anything "is," he must say it is to or of or in relation to something" (160b). This means that, in order to make sense in language, prior ontological analysis of reality is required. "Do they acknowledge further that the soul knows and Real being is known?"[19] (*Sophist*, 248d). They ought to, Plato thinks, since this is the "correct" conclusion. Words which mean something when put together do so because they reflect the structure of their object now transferred into the structure of language. Words which do not mean anything when strung together may be violating an internal law of language, a rule of grammar. However they also fail to reflect any structure to be found among real or possible entities.

---

[18] Plato, *Epistle VII*, trans. by Post, p. 95, Oxford, 1925.
[19] Plato, *Sophist*, trans. by Cornford, p. 305, Kegan Paul, London, 1949.

"And so, just as some things fit together and some do not, so with the signs of speech: some do not fit, but those that do fit make a statement" (262d). Only our apprehension of reality can tell us that words actually describe some possible thing when strung together. The distinction to be drawn here is this: between real or possible objects themselves and the way in which they relate to one another; and on the other side, language which attempts to participate in this relationship.

"Is there no difference between the names and the things which are signified by them?" (Augustine, op. cit., p. 13). The answer is that, for the sake of clarity, language must not be taken for its own object and confused with the independent objects of language. Unless we make this distinction and eventually direct our minds away from language structure toward its ontological object, we cannot discuss at all effectively together. Without reference to the structure of the real things themselves, the purpose behind the structure of language cannot be made evident.

Introversion, the solipsism Wittgenstein avoided, results unless when we hear words we direct the mind away from the symbols toward the thing of which they are the signs (p. 32). This is the only fruitful philosophical use of language, and our ability to treat language in an appropriate manner depends on our ability to discern the ontological status which it enjoys. Failing to achieve this prior realization, our skillful dissection of language will be to little avail, except perhaps to solve internally generated puzzles.

"Now then I wish you to understand that things which are signified are more to be depended on than signs..." (p. 35). "For you grant that the cognition of things is superior to the signs of things," (p. 37) Augustine asks.

6 Truth and Philosophical Theory

A. Philosophy Made Obvious?

In the *Tractatus* Wittgenstein thought that theory could become "truth itself"—except that so much of importance was left outside, and this could not be labeled "untruth," not even in Nietzsche's sense. But the propositions of the *Tractatus* pointed beyond themselves, so that it did not take long to revise the early "hard-line truth," to separate truth from theory (which he had begun to do at the end of the *Tractatus* by eliminating the steps that led him there). Now, theory can never itself "be" truth, at least not all truth, since reality lies beyond. But it may at least point to it, show it, as he came to say.

From the beginning, Wittgenstein's own problems bore little resemblance to the technical problems of logic, not that they should. Logic is a self-contained discipline. But he did not close it in on itself. Instead, from inside its structure he pointed to what logical propositions could not contain. Yet oddly, as he broke out of the logico-mathematical cage, instead of widening his early limited notion of philosophy in order now to take in his concerns, he did turn attention away from logic but only to the structure of language. We have discussed what, knowingly or unknowingly, might have attracted him to this (Chap. V). But he still could not give up the notion that all philosophy deals with "puzzles," which logicians do.

Wittgenstein became discouraged about the possibility of finality in math/logic, but in turning to language he still sought a "Modern" finality of method. This would not release him from his own problems, but "the professional philosopher" could achieve resolution. However, it is no wonder that the importance of philosophy, or at least of teaching philosophy, paled for him. It could dissolve itself but not human problems. What if only some problems, i.e., the abstract, technical ones, can be solved by examining language? What if those which are the most important can't? What if, as Rilke suggested, one has to learn to live and love the questions, not seeking answers? Yet Wittgenstein's intensity over technical issues never ceased. He could not turn off the logic machine.

The "new method" lies in simplifying philosophical questions and making them disappear as language confusion clears. All the while his own life is getting more and more complex. Philosophy thus seemed useless to him personally. Yet whether you "solve" or "dissolve" the questions of philosophy depends on what you take these questions to be. But can any method for approaching philosophy ever be held to be universal? The commonalty of techniques in mathematics offer a poor model for philosophy, and Wittgenstein did begin as a mathematical logician. He wanted to get rid of philosophy's first question, itself. But can that be done if our methods remain diverse?

What if some problems can be solved by the analysis of language and by studying language grammar but not all? Abstract, technical ones, trivial ones, perhaps. But what if the most important human ones cannot. Such truth, then, ironically lies outside theory. Wittgenstein is intently aware from the beginning that much lay outside what could be spoken of clearly. This would seem to mean that all philosophy's problems cannot be put within language, so that to direct philosophy to language is automatically to exclude the consideration of issues which do not, cannot, appear fully there. Thus, to concentrate on language is at once to leave major issues untouched, so that the method to "solve" philosophy's problems applies only to a limited range.

Final truth eludes philosophy, and it eluded Wittgenstein too. Within philosophy (as rigidly defined) all can be made quiet, left undisturbed. But with what should "philosophers" concern themselves? The attempt to confine attention to logical propositions could not succeed because the "system" left us staring at what it could not say and ready to abandon the easy steps which had led us to that point. Language, ordinary language, opens wide the gates, since "ordinary people" are not as afraid as logicians are to talk about what cannot be said precisely, clearly. In fact, they often speak just because they are trying to express what is most difficult to say.

However, the logician continues to pursue. He treats language as if it were the "games" logicians play, as if it contained only the "mental cramps" that mathematicians try to unravel and not every "song" known to man or woman. If truth is not identical with language, no analysis of language can solve philosophy's problems, that is, if philosophers are still seekers after the truth and not merely technicians.

Wittgenstein did come to want us to "live truth," to show what difference a theory, a doctrine, a belief, made in our actions. But then such a test of truth already lies outside the structure of language and no amount of examination of language will find it there—just because its enactment is not like a game.

Our issue is the relationship of logic, language to the fundamental problems of philosophy. Wittgenstein did not want mathematics reduced to logic. The *Tractatus* will not reduce philosophy to logic. The *Investigations* attempts, at times, to reduce philosophy to the analysis of language, but all the while his own concerns for truth are moving away from any test of words. Furthermore, as "ordinary" language opens wide, moving beyond the confines of logical structure, Wittgenstein himself is seeking truth elsewhere. He had discovered, invented, a new method for dealing with "philosophical questions," but it can be effective only if all of "truth" can be expressed within some language.

Sartre and Camus thought that the language used in plays and novels brought philosophical expression closer to truth. Wittgenstein did not write fiction, but he did find Dostoyevsky insightful as poetry and admitted it as a valid form of expression. Emotion appears more easily in such forms; language as analyzed seems dry. The Vienna Circle had ruled psychology outside philosophy, but that only solved philosophy's problems by stipulated definition. Wittgenstein did not accept that, but he never did find a method for dealing with emotions as effective as the one for dealing with vague expressions. In his own life Wittgenstein shifts away from logical proof and tests of clarity to pragmatics, how theory is lived and works in practice. We should, then, test his theories against the record of his life and what he himself had to say about it.

Remember: although Schopenhauer does not appear formally in his writings, Wittgenstein read *The World as Will and Idea* early on. We can call this an early "logical indiscretion" if we like, but the point is to remember Schopenhauer's idea that the only way to alleviate suffering, since it comes from the will's striving, is through the denial of the will. Does this give us any insight into Wittgenstein's abandoning wealth, living austerely and often in isolation? We know he suffered, experienced depression and thought of suicide. Was his ascetic practice a form of denial of the will where logic/language could not help?

What is the relationship between life's "problems" and philosophy's "problems"? How did this "show" itself in Wittgenstein's life? We know that his solutions to philosophy's puzzles did not solve anything in his own life. But he began as a mathematical logician, and logicians cannot be expected to feel that the internal puzzles of logical systems bear much relationship to personal questions. Wittgenstein turned away from logical systems to language, but he still saw it on the model of the "games" logicians play. These could perhaps be solved, mental traps unsprung, those caught in them released. But this turned philosophy back on itself as a technique, rather that out to the reality he knew from the beginning to lie outside the system.

Logic is a "game." We define the rules and everyone must know them in order to play. But language is not—or should not—be a "game." It does have grammar which linguists can explore, but no master of languages heretofore thought of himself/herself as solving philosophy's problems. True, there is the agonizing problem of translation from one language into another. This should be enough to let us see that meaning, much of it, stays locked within the language and that no technique can draw all of it out so that disagreements disappear. Meaning eludes common translation.

It is clear that what Wittgenstein wants is a solution to human problems. But logic/math/language cannot give him this, since they are each mentally erected structures, although language comes closest to human issues if it is not treated as a logical system. For instance, by admission both "love" and "God" concern Wittgenstein. But God in particular lies beyond language. Wittgenstein's increasing pragmatic bent tells him, in the words of the song, "don't talk about love, show me!" Belief can be analyzed in epistemology, and Wittgenstein cannot "believe" in God. But he does think God affects lives. Interestingly, Jesus did not say much about "believing" in God. He recommended that we "love" God with all our heart, etc. But the giving of love was precisely what was most difficult for Wittgenstein.

Words have power. Every writer knows, or hopes, that. But truth is more complex than words, and Wittgenstein knew from the beginning that much escaped propositions. So as he began his examinations of language, whatever he might discover, however illuminating language games might be, however much primitive language acquisition might tell us, it was already clear that language by far does not contain, could not contain, truth, i.e., all that is important for us to pursue. Powerful words can simplify complexity. That is the skill of the effective teacher/writer. But truth itself may not be as simple or capable of any final simplification.

Furthermore, what if there is an inner, an often hidden, voice of language? If this is true, a surface examination of the meaning of terms will never eliminate misunderstanding or insure mutual enlightenment. Of course, Wittgenstein spoke of depth analysis and more and more shunned surface analysis. But if so, how deep are the depths? Recall that Heidegger thought that all of Being lay hidden within language. We need not accuse Wittgenstein of "mystifying" language in this way. In fact, he was more careful than Heidegger, so careful as to shut the mystical outside language. But that was the language of the *Tractatus*. As those bounds are broken, does the mystical begin to appear within language again, as we have suggested.

Is there such a thing as "extra-ordinary" language as well as ordinary language? And are its games not so simple, not played within anyone's rules? Do we in fact look for, search out, non-ordinary phrases looking for insight there, so that comparisons with ordinary languages and the child's learning of language may be of little help to us there. "We put away childish things." Simple truth may lie in simple sentences. But the poetry of Blake is fascinatingly complex, but it does not yield to ordinary touch and it seems to escape final understanding. It may technically be "nonsense," but Wittgenstein never doubted that it was important.

B. Truth Made Easy?

According to either the *Tractatus* or the *Investigations*, to discover truth should be possible. It is rendered clear for us by either method. But all this does depend on whether we use the right method. Now, given the disappearing model of "universalism" in science, plus our final disillusionment over Modern Philosophy's confidence in "method" to solve philosophy's problems, truth cannot be "easy to discover" unless we all agree on one approach. The subtlety of Wittgenstein's second developed method is that it makes philosophical puzzles disappear. Philosophical practice dissolves its own need for itself. Still, this depends upon whether all of importance lies within in the conscious mind, which Freud has convinced us is not true.

Moreover, Wittgenstein hoped to eliminate philosophy's "first problem," i.e., itself, the constant need to define its mission. True, mathematicians do not spend much time in a quandary over what mathematics is or what it should do, although the issue can arise. That is philosophy's personal burden, and we know we are dealing with "philosophical" issues whenever we cannot all agree on how we should proceed. But for those who do not decide to follow Wittgenstein's methods, the result is that philosophy's problems are not solved and that its definition and approach may still be in question. In his practice, Wittgenstein knew that his method could not be easy or obvious, since he treated it as esoteric knowledge to be imparted only to the few and he feared its popularization.

As he defined it, the method cannot "solve" philosophical problems unless it is widely applied and universally accepted. So if it can be imparted only to the few ardent seekers, its "truth" will remain hidden, esoteric. Furthermore, if truth does lie hidden in language, what if some of it is beyond being rendered obvious, as Wittgenstein knew that the mystical was. Language analysis can apply only to what is within language, and some important truths may be too deeply hidden there to be exposed to all equally, or they may even lie outside the gates of language. Is truth, then, esoteric and not exoteric, as all of Modern Philosophy supposed (hoped)?

To be exoteric, truth must be apprehensible by all. Analysis of simple language games, ordinary language, might be, since it is both simple and ordinary. But is the method which will expose truth, or cause the mist to disappear—is the method itself esoteric, that is, not fully, perhaps never fully, understandable and so acceptable by all? If so, this amounts to truth itself being esoteric, partly hidden, open only to the few. For we know from the Empiricists, and from Descartes' clear and distinct ideas, that for truth to be final it must be open to all in the same way. If it has not been so in the past, we count on finding the "right method" now to rectify that shortcoming. For Wittgenstein the only major remaining problem can be symbolized by "God." Divinity is the opposite of a clear and distinct idea and lies outside the confines of all methodologies. And yet it may be important to final truth.

When we ask the question of whether truth can be made easy (we know it was never easy in Wittgenstein's life), we can go beyond considering Heidegger's hiding of Being in language, or Freud's unconscious, and consider Sartre's "self-deception." To lie, one must know the truth. That is easy to see when lying to another. You must know what is true in order to be able to lie effectively. But self-deception is lying to oneself and is more complicated, because you have hidden the truth from yourself. It is not a conscious lie. You have deceived yourself, not another. In language analysis, in language games, Wittgenstein has assumed that the problem of truth, philosophy's problem, lies external to ourselves; it concerns puzzles for us to open up which lie outside the mind.

What if the self is not so clearly known, does not even exist fully formed (which Kierkegaard asserted and whom Wittgenstein read)? Even more difficult, what if the self's most difficult problem is honesty with itself and that we may have hidden from ourselves things we must know if truth is to be discovered? Wittgenstein endorsed the Socratic maxim, "Know Thyself," and he knew it to be no simple matter in his own life. But perhaps his logical/mathematical background prevented him from seeing the importance of the person in truth-seeking and the way in which either the unstable (c.f. Kierkegaard's "sickness") or the self-deceived self can block all hope of uncovering truth finally, even should it lie "within language."

Seeking the truth, finding the truth, saying the truth—these may not be identical enterprises. To seek may not be to find, in spite of Jesus' words. Finding may not be the same as the ability to say the truth. And still beyond that, is "receiving the truth" something which no speaker of language can control? As the deaf man can turn off his hearing aid when he does not care to listen, is the reception of truth out of the control of the sayer (as Plato and Augustine thought), so that to find it in language would be far from the same as to make it heard or to assure its being received? Did Wittgenstein forget the human fact that truth can always be refused? In mathematics, in logic, this is not a major concern. In philosophy, it is the essence of the matter.

Wittgenstein thought that he had rejected British Empiricism. But did he in fact simply come to analyze language as others had analyzed sense experience? The color before one has a surface obviousness, even if it is hard to express precisely to everyone's agreement. But with language we begin far from the obvious, at a distance from our immediate sense experience. And its depths appear even more quickly than when Hume examined our knowledge of causation. True we do not "see" the cause; we see only our changed perceptions. However, where language is concerned, the comparison of seeing words to seeing colors is misleading. We are led immediately from surface impressions we all share to depths of the mind which defy our expression.

If language cannot be made clear and simple, as we had hoped our sense impressions could be, what happens to our standard of truth and to our notion of truth itself? We know that Wittgenstein hoped language could be made clear with the use of his method, philosophy itself made unnecessary, our mental cramps relieved, the fly let out of the fly bottle. But "reality" had been left outside the propositional system of the *Tractatus* as that to which propositions were compared to determine their truth. Thus, truth was not fully contained within the propositional system itself, however neatly that might be structured. This does not even include the mystical, which we know never can be brought "inside."

When the strict logical system of propositions is abandoned as philosophy's fortress, when language replaces it as philosophy's focus, can we theoretically render it as clear and as transparent as the set of propositions (although perhaps it is not so in fact)? But language itself is not the home of all truth. Reality—to which it must be compared—lies outside its limits, just as it did for the *Tractatus*. "God" is not proven by propositions. He is believed, altered in lived conduct. Words cannot exhibit that truth—or its denial—either. Like logic language has a tendency to introversion. One can be lost—or found—within its walls. But on the other hand, language always carries with it the question of its relation to reality, that which lies outside its walls.

Thus to simplify, to clarify language is not the same, or may not be the same, as to make what is true clear to us. Of course, the intricacy and the novelty and the power of Wittgenstein's suggested approach to language is that he feels the persons engaged in this pursuit will testify to the discovery of truth by the dissolution of that which perplexed them. However, the fact that we might "see" or experience this as happening by following one of Wittgenstein's explorations of a language game, this does not allow us to universalize and to say that the same enlightenment will come to all and in every situation of examining language use. True, procedures in logic and mathematics seem immediately universalizable. But the individuality of philosophy may distinguish it from logic at this crucial point.

To examine intricately, carefully, the structure and nuances of our language, detecting the rules of the games we play with it, this may always cause the player to worry (even after his or her linguistic worries dissolve) about the world outside of language introversion. Can we discover truth internally to language, other than merely grammar? Is its grammar identical to the structure of reality, or does it only overlap at points (we know grammar misses the mystical at least)? What role does the user of the language game play in the individual's own appraisal of truth? How "real" must we declare all that escapes language to be? Even if we simplify language to the ordinary and the primitive, might truth ironically grow even more complex and elusive than in the past?

C. The Philosopher's Task, a Suggested Contrast for Wittgenstein

The philosopher's task in the *Tractatus* is clear, but Wittgenstein moves beyond it. The philosopher's task in the *Investigations* and in the later writings is much harder to define with clarity and precision and has been taken slightly differently by different followers. What complicates the procedure is the fact that Wittgenstein was never direct and entirely clear about this, although his view of the philosopher's task emerges in a variety of comments. One problem is that there is some question as to whether the philosopher's business is to "work him/herself out of a job." Academic philosophy was not "high on Wittgenstein's list." And if his method were properly applied, philosophical problems would disappear—along with its professional exercise.

But since the issue of the concept of philosophy and its appropriate method is itself in question, let us use Plato by way of contrast and see how that might illuminate what one takes the work of philosophy to be. Plato offers us an enlightening contrast, since Wittgenstein moved more toward a dialogue method himself, and the basic work of exploring the meaning of vague terms is common to both. Oddly, however, Plato is often said to have projected to write a dialogue about the philosopher, which he did not do as such or explicitly; it is one we do not have. But very much as in Wittgenstein's case, we must ask: did Plato in fact describe the work of the philosopher by indirection as he worked on other questions?

It is somewhat ironic that Plato, who has written as much about the nature of philosophy and the philosophic life as any classical figure, should be thought to have left unwritten his description of the philosopher.[*] And yet the opinion of the scholars seems almost unanimous on this point, to the extent that all of their discussion centers around why he might have left this analysis of philosophy's task unwritten. The belief that the discussion of a philosopher is either missing or was left unwritten is particularly strange in that there is so much internal evidence within the Platonic writings to support the belief that Plato has written for us as complete a description of the philosopher's role as he believes it possible to set down in a final form. Like the later Wittgenstein, Plato seldom gives us any doctrine overtly. Thus, it should not be surprising, to one who understands the Platonic

---

[*] Note: Some material in this section comes from an article, "Plato, Unwritten Dialogue, The Philosopher" in *Proceedings of the XIIth International Congress of Philosophy*, Vol. II, Firenza, Italy, 1960, pp. 159-167.

method and spirit, to find that Plato actually has left us his discussion of the *Philosopher*, but that he has done this through his characteristic method of indirection, which was Kierkegaard's approach too.

All of the discussion about this supposedly unwritten dialogue rests on Plato's own reference to the subject in the opening passages of both the *Sophist* and the *Statesman*. However, it should be noted specifically that Plato nowhere says in so many words that he intends to write three separate dialogues. He merely proposes to discuss with the Stranger (217a) his opinion about the Sophist, statesman and philosopher, with the hope of arriving at a clear definition of the nature of each (217b). All that we can say is that two dialogues bearing two titles out of the three subjects proposed for discussion were written, but nothing tells us that the three topics could not be covered in two discussions. In fact, the assumption that the philosopher has been defined as precisely as is possible, but only indirectly and in the process of discussing two other professions, should of itself tell us something significant about the philosopher's role—that it would be impossible to convey through direct discussion.

In the opening passages of the *Statesman* reference is made to the completed discussion of the *Sophist*, indicating that two out of the three topics remain to be discussed, i.e., philosopher and statesman. The statesman is then selected as the topic for that discussion, but it is important to note that nowhere are we specifically told that the philosopher is not to be discussed. On the surface two topics are selected and a third postponed, but beneath this there is no passage which prevents the assumption that the third topic is also considered simultaneously in the process of the two discussions. In fact, there are several statements made by Plato which say almost exactly that. Discussion of the nature of the philosopher is not at all missing from these two dialogues. Perhaps then, an examination of the specific references to philosophy can provide as clear a picture of the one as it does of the other two. In fact, Plato's major point seems to be that the three are actually to be defined correlatively, so that if two can be considered as successfully defined, the third is automatically included. Let us look at this examination of the definition of the philosopher within the structure of the two dialogues, first with a consideration of the *Statesman* and then working back to the *Sophist*, which actually is the more important of the two for the description of the philosopher.

In his introduction to the *Statesman*,[1] Skemp takes it for granted that Plato's explicit plan was to produce the *Philosopher* as the fourth of the series, *Theaetetus, Sophist* and *Politicus* (p. 14). He goes on to surmise that Plato's third visit to Sicily caused him to abandon the actual writing (p. 17), thus giving a practical solution to the problem of the supposedly missing work, when the real solution may be theoretical. Having thus dismissed the issue without ever questioning whether Plato intended to produce a separate dialogue with the title *Philosopher*, Skemp does go on to characterize the Statesman as "an exercise in philosophical method" (p. 18). If the *Statesman* does in fact give us Plato's clearest statement about the philosophic method (and if, to jump ahead of the story, the *Sophist* gives us Plato's most precise analysis of the philosopher's object of analysis, i.e., being and non-being), then what reason have we to assume that this is not the best and most complete definition of the philosopher Plato could provide?

Skemp goes on to arrange the principal speakers in the four dialogues (*Theaetetus, Sophist, Statesman* and *Philosopher*) into a symmetrical pattern (p. 20) and to argue that the symmetry of the ordering argues for Plato's actual intent to write the *Philosopher*. This argument from the supposed perfect ordering of external structure seems rather weak, considering the apparent disconnection and lack of completion found in so many of the dialogues. Such ordering, even if it was actually worked out by Plato, could equally well argue that Plato explicitly set the stage for all of the pieces of the philosopher to be assembled but consciously left this as a task suited only to a reader, something Wittgenstein often did. Skemp agrees that Plato nowhere assumes that Philosopher, Statesman and Sophist are in fact three distinct types but instead leaves it an open question as to whether the three are really one. He then argues that they cannot be reduced to less than three types on the grounds that—there could be less only if philosopher and statesman were identical (p. 21). Yet it could be that while the philosopher is identical with neither statesman or Sophist, he cannot be defined in isolation (i.e., in some supposed uncompleted missing dialogue) precisely because a philosopher can be defined only by indirection as a byproduct of the discussion of statesman and Sophist. In defining these two points the third is defined automatically, for the one who has the eyes to see, that is, not universally for all.

---

[1] Plato's *Statesman*, trans. J.B. Skemp, Routledge & Kegan Paul, London, 1952.

In "searching out the statesman" the process is gone about by division, so that the procedure for defining the statesman certainly is the philosopher's business and tells us as much about him or her as it does about the statesman. We learn what a philosopher is by watching one in action, as Wittgenstein comes to agree, which we do in every Platonic dialogue and which is consciously stated in the *Statesman*. The philosopher must divide classes, not impulsively or arbitrarily, but only "if the structure of reality authorizes such immediate division" (262b). The task of the philosopher is to "distinguish more clearly between a mere portion and a true subdivision" (263a). In such abstract business examples shall be used, but they must be carefully chosen, since some can lead us astray rather than make the business of definition more easy. Measurement is involved in the philosopher's art and also in the structure of being.

Plato finally arrives at his most explicit statement of proper philosophical procedure:

> The following would be the right method. Wherever it is the essential *affinity* between a group of given forms which the philosopher perceives on first inspection, he ought not to forsake his task until he sees clearly as many true differences as exist within the whole complex unity—the differences which exist in reality and constitute the several species (285b).
>
> ...Until he has gathered together all the forms which are in fact cognate and has penned them safely in their common fold by comprehending them all in their real group (285d).

And then he asks the question which is crucial for our problem concerning the philosopher's task:

> Why did we set ourselves the problem? Is our chief purpose to find the Statesman, or have we the larger aim of becoming better philosophers, more able to tackle all questions (285d)?

What Plato seems to be telling us here is that, although his attempt to understand the statesman's art was genuine, you learn as much about the philosopher as you do about the statesman, since it is the philosopher whom we observe at work. "Doing precedes learning." In pure volume, much more is said about the philosopher's task of division, and the use of example and proper definition, than is actually concluded about the statesman. If Plato's sole aim was to define the statesman, he certainly could have done it not only more simply but also more directly. Instead, what we see is the philosopher's self-conscious reflection on the problems involved in his or her business of clearing up definitions.

It is also in the *Statesman* that Plato stresses the necessity for the philosopher to be trained to give and to receive a rational account, since he often deals with objects which are "...not to be apprehended by any other means" (286b). And then he seems to add the key as to how the discussion of the *Statesman* may be construed as defining the philosopher too: "All our present discussions have the aim of training us to apprehend this highest class of existents" (286b). The definition of the statesman can only be undertaken by a philosopher, and the problems encountered in definition by using the method of division tell us as much about the philosopher as about the statesman. What we really learn from the *Statesman* is a grasp of philosophical method, which is to have discovered the methodological half of our desired definition of the philosopher. "What we must value first and foremost, above all else, is the philosophical method itself, and this consists in the ability to divide according to real forms" (286e).

Does the *Sophist*, then, provide us with the other half of our desired definition of the philosopher, that is, of the primary object of the philosopher's skill? If so, the two dialogues will yield three definitions, and the dialogue on the philosopher will not prove to be unwritten, except in the most trivial sense that it does not appear separately, explicitly, and labeled as such.

In considering the question as to whether the *Philosopher* is missing or not, it is important to consider Plato's introduction of the Elean Stranger as "a real philosopher," (216a) together with the fact that he appears as a major speaker in these two dialogues only. It is a possible interpretation that his discussion of the two subjects of the statesman and the Sophist in itself adds the definition of the philosopher by example. Following his introduction, Socrates suggests that the stranger may be "a kind of god of refutation," (216b) but this answer seems to suggest, through irony, that philosophers are merely human and not at all extraordinary. They do "ordinary things," as Wittgenstein might say.

Perhaps even more important for our central question is Socrates' apparent summary of this opening conversation when he says that philosophers "appear in all sorts of shapes," (217c) sometimes as Sophists and sometimes as statesmen. Plato's meaning seems clear. Philosophers are not a separate class but reveal themselves to the discerning eye in the consideration of other professions. Philosophy, and philosophers, cannot be made explicit or obvious, but the eye can be trained to distinguish such people and their philosophical activity in reflecting upon the kind of process which we find in both the *Sophist* and *Statesman*—or in the *Investigations*.

Just as the attempt to define the Sophist begins with the definition of the angler, as an example which is easier to handle, so we might conclude that the definition of the philosopher is to be done indirectly by using the Sophist and statesman as examples. However, the difficulty in defining the Sophist quickly proves to be the difficulty of explaining "non-being." Falsehood must be explained in order to explain the Sophist, and this involves "the bold assumption that not-being exists, for otherwise falsehood could not come into existence" (237a). Not-being and being, and how not-being may be said to exist, must be understood in order to make the Sophist's art clear. But is not such a task exactly that of the philosopher? If the relation of not-being and being must be grasped, who else could understand the Sophist except one who is willing to become a philosopher?

It is not without significance that Plato chooses the *Sophist* as the place to give one of his most provocative definitions of existence, an undertaking which is certainly the philosopher's primary task.

> I suggest that everything which possesses any power of any kind, either to produce a change in anything of any nature or to be affected even in the least degree by the slightest cause, though it be only on one occasion, has real existence (247e).

Plato sets up the definition of being as "nothing else than power" (247e). This is certainly the center of the philosopher's proper interest. But more than this, in the *Sophist* he goes on to define what is "real" as both things in motion as well as things immovable (249d). Heretofore Plato has talked primarily as if only immovable things were "real" and that the motionless Forms defined being. Now he admits both the genuine reality of non-being and the changeable and moveable world as included in what we must admit to be real. In the *Sophist*, then, we have some of Plato's best thought of being and its modes, non-being, reality and existence. What other concerns could define the philosopher more clearly for Plato?

The *Sophist* reveals to us the difficulty of the inquiry about being, and "it is this difficulty which allows for both sophistry and genuine philosophy to result from a consideration of the same object" (251a). If being and non-being were not so perplexingly intertwined, neither would the definition of the Sophist yield the definition of the philosopher during the solution to the mixture. Because of this involvement, if either being or non-being "...emerges more dimly or more clearly, so will the other emerge" (251a). And the same seems to be true for the relation between the philosopher and the Sophist. Either the definition of the Sophist fails, or we see both more clearly as a result of making the relation between being and non-being more evident. Wittgenstein drew his definition of the philosopher first from mathematics and logic; later from language. And this derivation is crucial for understanding his struggle with "the mystical."

Plato next concludes what is probably the most direct, and certainly the most significant, statement for our problem. It seems so clear that it is hard to understand why it has not been accepted as Plato's own solution to the mystery of the supposedly missing statement about the philosopher: "Or, by Zeus, have we unwittingly stumbled upon the science that belongs to free men and perhaps found the philosopher while we were looking for the Sophist?" (253d). The question of the Sophist's art led to the problem of how non-being can be. And in the process of solving the perplexing status of non-being and being, existence and reality were defined. How can anyone avoid the conclusion that the search for the Sophist led to both the Sophist and the philosopher and that Plato intended it to be this way? What else could possibly be left for Plato to put in a dialogue entitled *Philosopher*? No one, except perhaps Plato, seems to have considered the fact that all the possible topics for the *Philosopher* have already been covered in other dialogues, and specifically in these two. We have been tricked by an announced title into overlooking the fact that there is no possible content left for such a possible dialogue. Wittgenstein might say that our philosophical dilemma had "dissolved." Even if Plato himself did intend at the outset to add such a dialogue (which seems doubtful), perhaps he discovered that he had already said all that he could possibly say on the subject.

However, this direct statement about the intricate relationship of philosopher to Sophist, mirroring the relationship of being and non-being, is only the beginning. Following this comes the important section about the mingling of forms, those that do blend and those that do not. "Dialectic," surely the Platonic philosopher's prime weapon, is defined as the division of things according to classes and the knowledge of what things can or cannot be associated with one another (253e). It is exactly here, Plato tells us, in this region that the philosopher will be found (254a). Next an even longer passage follows defining the philosopher and Sophist by contrast. The problem of being and non-being is the same for both he reports; only their relationship to it differs. The Sophist is distinguished by his tendency to run away into the darkness of non-being; but the philosopher devotes himself through reason to being and is hard to distinguish on account of the brilliant light (254b). What clearer definition of the philosopher, at least on Platonic terms, could anyone want?

The concepts of motion, rest, same and other, then undergo a dialectical analysis which at the same time illustrates the philosopher's procedure and defines the relation of being to non-being more clearly. Here Plato has surely passed from the consideration of the Sophist to an intricate definition of the philosopher and his task. The concept of "difference," Plato concludes (257b), seems to be a crucial concept to use in the analysis of being and non-being, and the not-being which explains the possibility of the Sophist's deception must be counted "as one class among the many classes of being" (258c). The presence of non-being within being, which is to be understood through the concept of "difference," allows the Sophist to hide, but it also defines the philosopher's problem. And Wittgenstein wants to expose "sophistry" too.

Thus, to understand the Sophist you must become a philosopher, because what is required is nothing less than an accurate understanding of the structure of being and of just how non-being can be present within it. Just as not-being is the opposite of being but is to be found distributed in all things, so the Sophist is not the opposite of the philosopher but is to be understood as a part of the philosopher's task (like the linguist and the philosopher for Wittgenstein?). The Sophist does not understand non-being to be a part of being but instead uses the obscurity of non-being to confuse others (and himself?). The philosopher must define precisely how non-being can be a part of being, so that in carrying out his job accurately he must come to understand, and thus to define, both the Sophist's art and his own. The Sophist tends to speak of things which are not as if they were, thus causing confusion through an improper perception of non-being. In contrast, the philosopher speaks of the relations between things which are, but in order to do this he must also define properly the sense in which everything involves things which are not, i.e., not-being, difference.

Thus, the philosopher must understand both himself and the Sophist, since the understanding of the Sophist is the understanding of how not-being can in some sense be. That is the definition of the philosopher's task. Plato could just as well have titled the *Sophist* the *Philosopher*, since the content of the dialogue would remain the same in either case. Plato's "unwritten" dialogue can be found written in the mind of every reader who understands the *Sophist* (and Plato) with any degree of sympathy and perception. In the same manner, the reader draws his or her own picture of the philosopher's task while reading the later Wittgenstein.

Although the problem surrounding the supposedly unwritten dialogue on the philosopher can be solved by an examination of two concrete members of the projected trilogy (i.e., *Sophist* and *Statesman*), the problem provides an interesting opportunity to review the rest of Plato's discussion on the nature of philosophy and the philosopher. Plato's dialogues, taken as a whole, contain innumerable references to this subject. In fact, it is no exaggeration to say that the nature of philosophy and the philosopher's art are in every dialogue, always at the forefront of Plato's thought. The dialogue method in itself reveals Plato's conception of the philosopher's art. His dialogues remain, as a body of literature, an instrument without parallel for the inculcation of the philosophical spirit into the philosophical novice.

The dialogue form is a method of indirection. In a like manner, Wittgenstein's late method teaches by indirection. This forever forbids saying dogmatically that "Plato (or Wittgenstein) believed this or that," for the simple truth is that Plato never himself speaks directly, whatever the changes in his dialogue technique may tell us about "Platonic philosophy." The statement that sets the scene for the discussion in the *Lysis* in many ways conveys the mood for every dialogue: this is a wrestling school "and our pastime chiefly consists of discussion" (204a). No reader can get a philosophical doctrine out of Plato without wrestling for it. Wittgenstein worried about "easy" students too, anyone who sought answers from him. The *Lysis*, like almost all of the "early dialogues," seems to have as its main target any person who claims to have answers to important questions either too easily or too certainly.

In the *Protagoras* Plato stresses the analogy of philosophy with medicine, as being an art or skill requiring precise knowledge. However, Plato is equally capable of parodying philosophy, if it becomes trivial and pointless as it does at one stage of the *Euthydemus*. Like the carver, the significant philosopher ought to have sharp instruments at his disposal and wield them according to an exact knowledge of the anatomy of his subject, as Plato remarks at one point in the *Cratylus* (387b).

The *Phaedrus* has traditionally been considered the home of much of Plato's direct statement about the life and goals of the philosopher. This is true, provided that the statements are considered in their context and not seized on too literally. The soul that has glimpsed the most on its journey through the world of the Forms is said to be born in the philosopher, and the synonym for philosopher is "lover of beauty," (248d) or one of a musical or a loving nature. (Recall Wittgenstein's attraction to music.) Phaedrus is warned that no one will ever be able to speak properly about anything unless he pays attention to philosophy (261a), and the business of philosophical distinction is again compared to the art and the skill required in good carving. In dividing by classes, the philosopher is the one who is able to recognize where the "natural joints" (265e) are. Plato rejects the epithet "wise" and prefers for the philosopher the more modest and more fitting title of "lover of wisdom" (278d). Such a philosophic life requires an inborn instinct (279b). One who loves never fully possesses.

In the *Symposium* the philosopher climbs the ladder of beauty, which alone leads him to insights. In the *Apology* the true philosopher is enjoined, like Socrates, to "fulfill the philosopher's mission" (29) of searching into himself and other human beings. Cross-examining is a duty for the serious philosopher, and this is an occupation which he or she ought not to abandon as long as he has life and strength (33) (c.f., Wittgenstein's sense of honesty and duty). The symbolic meaning of the philosopher's desire to "follow after the dying" (*Phaedo*, 62d) has been commented on many times. Probably the philosopher's supposed detachment from mundane pursuits is exaggerated by Plato's examples, especially in the light of other statements in the dialogues. But a philosopher certainly ought not to fear death the way another person might. He or she ought always to recognize the essentially intangible nature of our professional goals.

In the *Gorgias* philosophy is distinguished from rhetoric, which is "a producer of persuasion" (453a). And in the *Republic* Plato again returns to his favorite analogy for proper philosophic method, i.e., the trained physician's art. Like the physician, the philosopher studies the patient's interests, not his own. Rhythm and harmony, too, are important to the philosopher's art. They are a preparation for the coming of reason, and the love of beauty conduces to the same end. The genuine philosopher can only be one who has a genuine passion to see the truth (see Monk: "The Duty of Genius").

However, most important of all is Plato's unequivocal demand that philosophy be made powerful by uniting it with the statesman's skill, which is another evidence as to why a thorough inquiry into the statesman's art necessarily leads us to the philosopher too. The philosopher cannot be the powerless passenger on the ship, possessing a true knowledge of the skill of navigation all the while the ship founders. Nor can the philosopher be allowed to stand gazing at the sun after finding his way out of the cave of common experience (see the *Republic*).

Instead of standing drunk with his own new found wisdom, he or she must be forced to re-enter the cave and attempt the guidance of ordinary people. Such a task requires skill and power, in addition to knowledge. The power to approach Beauty, and to behold it as it is in itself, is rare indeed. Rarer still is the ability to translate such a perception into action. Yet this is unquestionably the Platonic philosopher's goal. "Philosophers" are those who are also able to apprehend the eternal and unchanging, and in every case their affections must be set on the reality, vs. opinion and appearance. Wittgenstein also thought that philosophical truth showed itself in action.

Since Plato describes how philosophic natures are corrupted by the acclaim of the multitude, it is easy to see that he held no brief on the necessity of pursuing philosophy. (He was as skeptical as Wittgenstein about most professors of philosophy.) The *Republic* also declares the multitude to be unfit for philosophy, so that we know that philosophy will always be the work of a few. Dialectic, as the *Republic* describes it, is surely the Platonic philosopher's tool, and this same method is at work in the *Statesman* and *Sophist* and so makes them more centrally philosophical than the surface topics might indicate. Finally, the *Republic* ends by showing the decline of the philosophic spirit and its final transformation into its opposite, despotism. Thus, in sheer content and straight forward account, as it so often does, the *Republic* contains a great deal of Platonic doctrine, this time concerning philosophy and the philosopher.

The *Parmenides* is one of the most difficult dialogues to place, and yet Plato hints that comprehending it is crucial in understanding the philosopher's job. "For many do not know that except by this devious passage through all things the mind cannot attain to the truth" (136e). Being able to grasp and to reproduce this complicated dialectic on the one and the many is necessary, then, for any true philosophical life. As the *Theatetus* tells us, the discovery of knowledge is not a small matter but a "task for the very ablest men" (148e). And it is here that Plato makes his famous statement about the necessity for a feeling of wonder if you are to be a philosopher, "since wonder is the only beginning of philosophy" (155d).

Philosophy deals for the most part with what cannot be immediately grasped with our hands. Thus, the philosopher must first of all train himself/herself for abstraction, affirming the existence of "actions and generation and all that is invisible" (155e) (c.f. Wittgenstein and logic.) The opposite of this sensitive spirit, that is, hostile and combative argument, makes some people come to hate philosophy (168a). Because of the necessary lack of concreteness, the philosopher often seems to appear ridiculous in practical settings, in the most part due to the constant perplexity in which we find ourselves. (Wittgenstein once hoped to offer us release.) In the *Statesman* Plato takes up this theme again:

> Therefore we must train ourselves to give and to understand a rational account of every existent thing. For the existents which have no visible embodiments, the existents which are of highest value and chief importance, are demonstrable by reason and not to be apprehended by any other means. All our present discussions have the aim of training us to apprehend this highest class of existents (286b).

Thus, all of the dialogues are a training ground for philosophy and an illustration of the philosopher's art and nature. But none more directly and avowedly so than the *Sophist* and *Statesman*. The examples given above are but a few of the myriad of statements to be found in the dialogues concerning the philosopher's task, indicating Plato's almost constant preoccupation with the topic. (An issue Wittgenstein hoped to dissolve.) Of course, Plato's own discussion in the famous VIIth epistle about the impossibility of kindling the spark of philosophy in anyone else, and Plato's reticence about putting his most profound thoughts into concrete and direct terms, might seem to work against this current thesis of seeing the *Sophist* and the *Statesman* as also giving us a definition of the Philosopher.

However, Plato's method is still indirect enough not to make his central thought too open to direct view, which the age old disagreement of students of Plato over the supposedly missing dialogue indicates all too abundantly. Plato's *Philosopher* is there, but not open to the direct and obvious view of all. Rather, "acquaintance with it must come... after a long period of attendance on instruction... when, suddenly, like a blaze kindled by a leaping spark, it is generated in the soul and at once becomes self-sustaining" (341d). Wittgenstein can and did strike the same spark for many.

7 PHILOSOPHY, SIMPLICITY, ASCETIC PRACTICE, AND LOVE

A. THE GOSPEL ACCORDING TO TOLSTOY

What did Wittgenstein find in reading Tolstoy's *Gospel in Brief* that, as Monk tells it, made such a profound and transforming impression on him? Monk does not report what the discovery was, only its effect. Wittgenstein admired Tolstoy's moral teachings (Monk, p. 342). He liked "Tolstoy's art," i.e., "art that is intelligible to everyone, and that espouses Christian virtues" (p. 569). This outlines an interesting connection between universal intelligibility and virtue, two factors which absorbed much of Wittgenstein's life and work. He thought so much of the *Gospel in Brief* that he gave it as presents (p. 213). He reported to others: "At its time, this book virtually kept me alive" (p. 132).

When he first began to read Tolstoy's *Gospel* he remarked: "I am on the path to a great discovery. But will I reach it?" (p. 117). The book had captivated him. "It became for him a kind of talisman; he carried it wherever he went and read it so often that he came to know whole passages by heart. He was known to his comrades as "the man with the gospels." For a time he "... became not only a believer, but an evangelist recommending Tolstoy's *Gospel* to anyone in distress" (p. 115-16). Wittgenstein's "duty to oneself" transformed his work into a curious hybrid, "combining as it does logical theory with religious mysticism," Monk concludes (p. 115-16).

What is "the gospel according to Tolstoy?"[1] It is: "...that the truth is to be found in the Christian teaching" (p. 367). But this means "an exposition of the real meaning of the Christian teaching." But what is

---

[1] *The Complete Works of Count Tolstoy*, Vol. XV, "Short Exposition of the Gospel," AMS Press, New York, 1968.

the meaning that is to be found in the gospel words? "The gratification of one's will is not necessary to one's life," (p. 368) and this can be seen as a principle which governed much of Wittgenstein's ascetic practice. But when Tolstoy comes to outline his method to find the truth in the gospels, he reports: "The main proof of the truth of the understanding is the unity, clearness, simplicity, fullness of the teaching, and its correspondence with the inner feeling of every man who is seeking the truth" (p. 371).

This outline throws some light on Wittgenstein's own later method, but Tolstoy becomes even clearer on this subject. What he complains about is the way interpreters and expositors and churches have confused our perception. In asking about the meaning of life, Tolstoy was brought to the point of despair and suicide (p. 374). He found all traditional teachings and doctrine like pearls mixed with mud. Then he found the source of light in the gospels and received "full answers to my questions about the meaning of my life" (p. 374). "The more indubitable did the difference between truth and untruth become to me" (p. 375).

What caused these "false" interpretations which distorted the teachings? The biblical commentators tried to harmonize what could not be harmonized, that is, not the gospels themselves, but the vast weight of all the interpretations and church teachings. One must not look to the massive commentary but at the simple words themselves. "The teaching of a great man is great in that it unites all in one truth," (p. 378) he concludes. Wittgenstein is also seeking clarity, truth and certainty, and an escape from the vast accumulation of the history of philosophy. Yet his writings show almost no footnotes or attempts to deal with past philosophers. Why? Because accumulated doctrines obscure. "The question is not to prove that Jesus was not God [Tolstoy commenting on Renan] ...but to understand wherein the teaching consisted" (p. 383).

Christianity, Tolstoy finds, is "a very strict, pure, and complete metaphysical and aesthetic teaching above which human reason has not risen" (p. 384). Churches do not expound it, he is convinced, and Wittgenstein became suspicious of universities and professors of philosophy, too. His reading of Tolstoy came at a time when Wittgenstein was trying to say that philosophical truth has been overlaid but that it could be "strict, pure, and complete" and "unite all men." To do this requires leaving the vast commentaries of philosophy behind and finding a direct method to interpret the text. At first this was the *Tractatus*, later the *Investigations*.

The parallels in Wittgenstein's and Tolstoy's lives are interesting. Both were born to wealth and prominence. Both knew strict and formalized churches with dogmatic teachings. Both became alienated from their religious background but never gave up their personal interest. However, Tolstoy was reconverted by his personal reading, while for Wittgenstein this happened momentarily, it seems, but never came to a permanent commitment. However, both left lavish lifestyles for a more ascetic practice, and both attacked what they considered to be institutions that obscured truth. However, Tolstoy rediscovered his religious conviction; Wittgenstein did not, in spite of his lifestyle which mirrored the monk's spiritual search.

Quite remarkably, when Tolstoy speaks about his method of approach, one passage sounds almost like Wittgenstein: "And when I comprehend these words, in the manner in which they were said, everything which had been dark became clear, and what seemed exaggerated became entirely clear" (p. 13, Vol. 16, in "My Religion"). And: "I do not wish to interpret Christ's teaching; the one thing I want is to prevent men from interpreting it" (p. 4). Wittgenstein wants to let everything stand untouched too. Tolstoy appeals to the understanding of "millions of simple, unwise men," (p. 4) in a very close parallel to "ordinary language." This method led to "a sudden removal of everything which concealed the very meaning of the teaching, and a sudden illumination by the light of the truth" (p. 6). Truth can be found in simple language, as it was for Wittgenstein too.

Speaking of a verse in Matthew, Tolstoy reports his new method of reading made him understand it "in its direct and simple meaning" (p. 11). Tolstoy claims he has no teaching of his own. Layers of interpretation have caused the blocks to our understanding. He simply understands it now as it was expounded. In order to do this, he tells us, do not interpret, but "understand them just as they are written (p. 483, Vol. 22, in "How To Read the Gospels"). "On the main things all men will be sure to agree, and one and the same thing will appear completely comprehensible to all" (pp. 484-85). In order to understand, "it is necessary... to sift in it what is fully comprehensible and simple from what is incomprehensible and complicated and...read what is clear and comprehensible... trying to become familiar with the meaning of the simple, clear teaching" (pp. 484-85).

Tolstoy's great discovery on how to read the gospels, so as to discover their clear truth, bears an amazing similarity to Wittgenstein's later proposal on how to solve philosophical differences. In the major work, "The Four Gospels Harmonized" from which *The Gospels in Brief* is drawn, Tolstoy reveals his strong belief in a rationalism which leads to universal agreement. Ironically, Wittgenstein mirrors this but adds to it a mysticism that is missing in Tolstoy. The answer to the meaning of life for Tolstoy "must be intelligible and must not contradict the laws of reason" (p. 11, Vol. 14). However, the answer comes first by revelation, not reason.

Tolstoy says that any "answer" is useless unless it answers his question about the meaning of life. Wittgenstein mirrors this quest for a clear certainty, but he never found the personal answer Tolstoy did, except for brief periods. Wittgenstein was taken by Augustine's *Confessions*, and adopted some of that style; Tolstoy wrote his *Confessions* too (Vol. 13). He found the religious teachings of the Orthodox church to be far from life. One should be able to find out if a man is a believer or not from his acts, but Tolstoy found only doctrine preached in churches. Yet as his faith faded, his real belief became a belief in perfection. "I tried to perfect myself mentally" (p. 7). "I tried to perfect my will and formed rules which I tried to follow" (p. 7).

As conventional faith evaporates, Tolstoy kept his search for moral rigor and the intense demand which this placed on him, as did Wittgenstein. His "gospel" became his discovery of how to see the words in scripture clear and free of confusing jargon, and his manner for accomplishing this bears striking similarities to Wittgenstein's. But Tolstoy's gospel also centered in love. "Not to deviate from the principle of his life... the beneficence of love" (p. 389, Vol. 15, in "Conclusion To a Short Exposition of the Gospel"). A man must sacrifice personal lusts, all his carnal life, "for the principle of beneficent love for his neighbors" (p. 389). "Our life has become love and is freed from fear and from all sufferings" (p. 393). So he summarizes his gospel.

B. THE GOSPEL ACCORDING TO WITTGENSTEIN

"Gospel" means essentially "the good news." Tolstoy clearly discovered the "good news" in his form of understanding the Gospels, and he offered this to all as a way to clear up centuries of unclarity and uncertainty. Wittgenstein, we know, not only read this proclamation but was profoundly impressed by it. However, his "good news" was intended essentially only for philosophers. It bears remarkable similarities to Tolstoy's, first, in its claim to have discovered clarity in texts obscured for centuries, second, as a method that provides a basis for universal agreement rather than difference over interpretations and, most important finally, a way of interpreting texts which relieved perplexity and mental pain.

We know that Wittgenstein never surrendered his interest in religion, specifically in Christianity. Like Tolstoy he came to affirm that "belief" was evidenced, "shown" primarily in action not in intellectual profession. Truth was there to be seen; the question was which approach could manifest this. The *Tractatus'* method was to create a propositional system of clarity and finality, a "Philosophy Without Ambiguity." Logic and mathematics allowed him to do this. These were his early methods, and they were just as ladened with history and myriad interpretations as Tolstoy found Christianity to be. Yet for Wittgenstein this was never all; the system was not self-contained. Outside it lay much of importance which was not surrendered to it, the mysterious.

Rejecting the narrowing of every concern to the restricted and constructed definition of "philosophy" which the Vienna Circle held to, Wittgenstein more and more felt the impact of all that lay outside the confines of the *Tractatus*. This forced him to revise his conception of "philosophy" so as not to exclude so much by simple definition. But interestingly enough, he did not surrender his search for final clarity He insisted on the possibility of agreement among philosophers and for a certainty in approach if not in systematic constructions. Like Tolstoy he wanted to eliminate the distress that differing interpretations, and dogmatic conflicts, had placed upon philosophers. As Tolstoy eliminates church dogmatics so Wittgenstein eliminates systematic construction, e.g., "metaphysics."

The vagueness of philosophy is now eliminated, just as the confusing quarrels over the meaning of the gospels were for Tolstoy. The way Tolstoy came surprisingly to understand the complexity of the Gospels after centuries of quarrels and disagreements is the same, or at least quite similar to, the way Wittgenstein comes to see the simplicity of truth in examining language, not that of the scholars and systematizers but of ordinary people. However similar the technique may be—and it is astounding—Wittgenstein omits the core of Tolstoy's "gospel": the beneficence of love and the way this frees life from fear and from suffering.

This is not to say that Wittgenstein did not recognize this in Tolstoy's discovery as the heart of the gospel that lay under centuries of scholarly commentary. It would be hard to say that anything consumed Wittgenstein's personal life more than the search for love. But he did accept Tolstoy's requirement that the gratification of one's will had to be sacrificed, which fits Wittgenstein's early reading of *The World as Will and Idea*. This involves extinguishing the will by ascetic practice, which he continually tried to do, although he never quite succeeded. One can easily say that his intellect was too strong to allow this, although he was painfully aware of this tension.

Tolstoy was not merely a "seeker after wisdom." He became a possessor of truth not merely a lover of or seeker after wisdom. He had found the method for certainty of insight. Wittgenstein never saw philosophy in its ancient guise, as a quest for knowledge without ever claiming to be wise. He started as a child of Modern Philosophy intent upon fixing the path to finality. The development of mathematical logic gave him even stronger reasons to think truth could be established vs. the rather meager introspection available to Descartes from his medieval heritage. Yet too much was left outside the clarity of the *Tractatus* to allow Wittgenstein to be satisfied.

If traditionally the philosopher is the one who knows that he or she lacks final knowledge and so claims only to have seen enough of it to know that it is desired, then Wittgenstein went beyond this uncertainty at least twice in his professional life. He found a way he thought could complete philosophy's task, even if it meant rendering philosophy no longer necessary. Yet his biography reflects little of this. Rather it shows us the more traditional philosophical odyssey, plus the religious pursuit of the moral life and the monk's quest for the mystical. That he found a key in Tolstoy that proved important to him philosophically may also tell us why it was not as satisfactory for him personally as it was for Tolstoy.

Jesus told his disciples that he who seeks to save his life shall lose it, and Tolstoy points to the key of the gospels as a beneficent love of neighbors. Yet it was the need of love that primarily blocked Wittgenstein's personal life. An ascetic and stringent ethical bent made him withdraw from sensual satisfaction, although it meant much to him. He knows not only that this is not equivalent to love but that sensuality might destroy it. So he withdraws. He also knows that love is given only as a gift, as a grace. Wittgenstein never experienced love in this self-giving, unselfish way. Tolstoy does seem somehow to have experienced the central message of love.

Philosophy, intellect, simplicity, ascetic practice and the search for love, all fought continually as competing goals in Wittgenstein's mind and soul, and they did so without resolution. There was a resolution, in a sense, in his later developed philosophical method of analysis of ordinary language. But if it released the fly of perplexity from the fly bottle of intricate metaphysics, we know that Wittgenstein never found release or knew the gift of love that seemed to give Tolstoy freedom. In fact freedom from his intellect as a taskmaster—this is precisely what he never knew. It was, as he says, at the same time his single talent and his most perplexing demand.

If philosophy is now open to consider all "language games" and ordinary languages, we know that much of the mystical can be found there, that which Wittgenstein recognized but shut out of the *Tractatus* for fear of its damage to the desired certainty. The method practiced in the *Investigations* and all the later writings shuts out nothing from being voiced in words. The issue becomes whether, if this is so, the method itself can rid us of perplexities. Can it take away nothing, leave everything as it was, except remove our perplexity, bring us into agreement and make further speculation in philosophy unnecessary? The method might accomplish this, but only if it is widely practiced and found personally rewarding by all.

Of course, his method has gained world-wide acceptance, in at least some circles. But Wittgenstein feared that his approach would be dogmatized, trivialized by his followers, from whom he distanced himself. If the method cannot be rigidified, then it cannot yield the desired conformity of procedure (as the ex-Marxist knows). However, more than this, it is clear that Wittgenstein never identified his professional life as a philosopher with the normal trappings of academe. He fought for something else than intellect in his personal life. His ascetic practice, his Spartan lifestyle, was one instrument. Yet much as he drove himself to this, it did not reconcile him with his need for love.

Lest the reader say that "love" is not a philosophical matter, we need to refer to "the love of wisdom," that is, desire, as being both crucial and central to philosophy's pursuit. Plato's account (among others) points out the necessity for love as the inspiration needed to break down mental barriers and carry us to new insights. Wittgenstein actually saw philosophy in its wider meaning, but his logical/mathematical training, plus the fire of his intellect in these matters, prevented him from broadening the actual goals of philosophy. He did open it to ordinary language, which could include examining "love" as much as "color," but he could not abandon finality and let love mean simply "the constant quest."

Wittgenstein, as we know, wanted to eliminate philosophy's "first question," that is, What is Philosophy? It is clear that, as long as this remains primal, certainty can neither characterize philosophy, because another definition of its task always remains possible, nor can finality become possible in philosophy other than by stipulating its definition thus arbitrarily shutting out whatever threatens finality. In the *Tractatus*, Wittgenstein took the later course, but he jeopardized its completion because he recognized all that was important outside, e.g., the mystical. The approach of the *Investigations* is more subtle.

That method allows anything said in language to be examined (although it still leaves out what cannot be said). But the pursuit of language games and the insights of ordinary language relieve the philosopher's perplexity and in that sense eliminates the need for philosophy itself. The ladder used to get to the insight is removed in ways different from that which the *Tractatus* suggested. But: what if one either does not accept "language" and its functions as Wittgenstein sees it (see V.C.) or does not accept the offered methodological approach? That many have is not the issue. Other methods remain possible; some perhaps are still undiscovered.

Also, if examinations are limited to ordinary expressions, have we treated all that appears in language? Consider *The Zohar*, "The Book of Splendor."[2] Wittgenstein has never denied the presence of "the mystical," and these are writings which express the mystical, "a work of secret wisdom" (p. 7). Thus, to test the methodology of clarifying language, we should examine language when it is not talking about "color" but about mystical concepts (and there are such) which are "expressed rather arbitrarily in new word-formations" (p. 27).

Even more difficult to appraise is this fact which Scholem reports about the *Zohar*: "that the effect upon the soul of such a work is in the end not at all dependent upon its being understood" (p. 9). This is hard for any critical method of the Enlightenment to accept, since the first premise of both Rationalism and Empiricism is that we will be greatly benefited by their efforts at clarification. Wittgenstein cannot reject this claim about the language of the *Zohar*, that its effect does not depend on understanding. He himself has said a belief will be judged by its effect upon a person, not by truth in a formula. So language clarification must proceed cautiously if in fact understanding is not necessary for beneficial effects to be produced at least in some cases. Some instances could prove

---

[2] Ed. Gershom G. Scholem, Schocken Books, New York, 1963.

to be detrimental, it is true, but still we must be cautious about the drive to clarify lest it eliminate too much of importance to us.

Furthermore, it is a touch ironic that the followers of Wittgenstein have taken on the enthusiasm of having a religious conviction, of finding a revelation which transforms one's outlook. We can now recognize that Wittgenstein's own transforming experience might have come from following Tolstoy's "gospel." This accounts for some of the non-dispassionate manner of both Wittgenstein and at least some of his followers. Like Luther, theirs is a "Reformation" movement. If so, one does not treat Wittgenstein as simply one among history's many insightful philosophers but as the spring of "new wine" that cannot be contained in "old wine bottles." Treating Wittgenstein's life and work as a gospel, as a "good news" helps to understand why "the mystical" could not be shut out, just as any Christian, Jew or Muslim can never forget Jesus, Moses or Mohammed, and why Wittgenstein so often has a "guru" status among his followers.

8 THE OMISSION OF ETHICS, THE EXCLUSION OF THEOLOGY*

A. THE DECLINE OF BRITISH ETHICAL THEORY [1]

(1) Ethical theory as an indicator of the health of philosophy.

Prichard's sentiment expressed in 1912 seems quite pertinent today: "Probably to most students of Moral philosophy there comes a time when they feel a vague sense of dissatisfaction with the whole subject" (p. 149). Surely everyone familiar with the history of philosophy in its broader context has been perplexed by following ethical discussions in England. To one not captured completely by this tradition, the ethical writing of the eighty years after Prichard's comment has a slightly peculiar ring. A change took place in the tenor of the discussion which made it different from that of the decades before. The unsatisfactory discussions that followed lead one to wonder whether the whole enterprise somehow got off on the wrong foot.

Some of the influential essays in ethical theory of the period from 1903 to 1951 have been collected under one cover.[2] The condensation and rapid juxtaposition of the results of nearly half a century of debate makes the direction of this period stand out from the specific issues. As the editors state, their "....aim has been to provide a balanced and

---

* Note: Some material in this section comes from an article, "Plato, Unwritten Dialogue, The Philosopher" in *Proceedings of the XIIth International Congress of Philosophy*, Vol. II, Firenza, Italy, 1960, pp. 159-167.
[1] Revised from an article which appeared in *Philosophy and Phenomenological Research*, Vol. XVIII, No. 2, Dec. 1957, pp. 219-227.
[2] All page references are to the volume Sellars and Hospers, *Readings in Ethical Theory*, New York: Appleton-Century-Crofts, 1952. The title and original place of publication of the various essays have been omitted for the sake of simplicity, since the individual articles are not the subject matter of this discussion. The focus here is on the collection as a whole as representative of an era, one in which Wittgenstein himself was active.

firsthand account of the theoretical controversies that have developed in ethics since the publication in 1903 of Moore's *Principia Ethica*" (p. ix). Read as a flashback into the recent past, such a collection helps to bring a busy half-century into focus. Our consideration aims now to relate to Wittgenstein's work certain lessons learned from this review.

Such an attempt to review the general direction of ethical discussion is important to more than moral theory itself. Philosophy's point of contact with the everyday world is primarily through ethical theory, as Wittgenstein felt. Thus, the health of philosophy as a whole is often evidenced by the fruitfulness of its ethical discussion. In spite of their technical sophistication, philosophers have never been able to ignore their early motto: "Vain is the word of the philosopher which does not heal any suffering of man" (Epictetus: Fragment 54). If a philosophical school is unable to make contact with the world through an ethical theory of some vitality, we cannot call the school "wrong" in its approach, but its moral theories are likely to be irrelevant and perhaps trivial. Thus, if a new line of philosophical inquiry is not destined to be fruitful, its sterility is most likely to be evidenced in its ethical inadequacy. Wittgenstein felt the exclusion of ethics from philosophy keenly and agonized over it.

(2) The curious ambivalence: theory and practice, action and meaning, the good and its definition.

The thesis of this appraisal is that although British ethical theory began with a real concern for conduct as well as an interest in analysis as a method, it gradually came to center upon questions of definition and paid mere lip service to the centrality of moral experience. In order to understand moral problems, early writers of this century started with an attempt at careful analysis and clear definition. Gradually, later writers tended to spend more time on these preliminaries, until they ended with little but the linguistic analysis. In the beginning the analysis of ethical language was a means; later it tended to become an end in itself. At first the analysis was judged by its ability to throw light on the complexities of the moral life. Eventually the method became its own internal judge, and ethical writing was called "significant" because of its internal clarity as a piece of analysis.

This concentration upon analysis and method, involving terms from the moral life but not the moral life itself, must have existed potentially in the original statement of the problem at the turn of the century. And here a curious ambivalence is to be noted. The early writers had the moral fervor characteristic of their time. But although they stressed practice and action and moral rightness, at the same time they unanimously agreed that ethics was a theoretical affair, and they spent increasing energy upon meaning and definition. The history of recent discussion cannot be understood without recognizing this original ambivalence. As the years passed, newer men dropped this double intention and wholeheartedly stressed analysis. But as this happened what must be asked is: did the ethical discussion lose most of its ethical import?

As everyone agrees, the discussion was given its direction largely by Moore's early assertions about the indefinability of good. Moore began by recommending the analysis and distinction of questions as a healthy preliminary. Taken by themselves, his words have a very contemporary ring.

> I do not know how far this source of error would be done away, if philosophers would try to discover what questions they were asking, before they set about to answer it: for the work of analysis and distinction is often very difficult (p. 53).

Wittgenstein said something of the same thing in stronger terms. Yet Moore follows this be reaffirming the centrality of conduct to philosophical ethics:

> They are all of them (ethical judgments) concerned with the question of "conduct"—with the question, what, in the conduct of us, human beings, is good, and what is bad, what is right and what is wrong (p. 66).

Moore asked two questions: "What... is good? How is good defined?" (p. 69). What foretells the future of the next half-century of discussion is that, although Moore begins with two questions, he spends more time on the second question of definition. Thus, with the passage of time those who follow after Moore drop the first question of "What is good?" Our intent is not to try to add to the long discussion of the definability of good, but to illustrate how the focus of the argument shifted from issues related to conduct toward a more or less intramural philosophical discussion, the debates of which have little to do with action.

Moore states that "as great part of the vast disagreement prevalent in Ethics is to be attributed to this failure in analysis" (p. 84). What he accomplishes is to shift the attention from conduct to an interest in the properties of terms. The question of what properties certain terms have has become a classical, a logical, and a general philosophical problem. But how this comes to be substituted for an ethical discussion of action is a strange affair. Moore has a great deal to do with this substitution when he states:

> The peculiarity of Ethics is not that it investigates assertions about human conduct but that it investigates assertions about the properties of things which is denoted by the term "good" and the converse property denoted by the term "bad" (p. 91).

Ethics is already once removed from actuality when it deals with assertions about human conduct. But a study of the properties of terms is surely twice removed and, moreover, is in danger of losing all direct connection with conduct.

In *The Methods of Ethics* Sidgwick echoes this demand for clarity and definition: "Let us begin by defining the issue raised as clearly as possible" (p. 137). It is interesting that both the moralists of the earlier period and present-day analysis share this striving for clarity and precision in definition. What has been lost is the moral aim toward which this striving was originally directed. Clarity and precision in definition were proposed as philosophical standards for a purpose. To be clear about trivial matters does not advance the moral life. It is true that in 1910 Russell states firmly that ethics is conceived as

> ...dealing with human conduct, and as deciding what is vicious among the kinds of conduct between which, in practice, people are called upon to choose (p. 1).

Yet the shift appears here again, when just a few lines later Russell adds that "The aim is, not practice, but propositions about practice" (p. 1). From practice to propositions about practice, and from there to propositions about the propositions of other philosophers—these are easy steps in which a great deal that is of importance may be lost.

When Moore discusses Utilitarianism in 1912, he begins by a statement which firmly links the enterprise of philosophy with the moral life:

> Can we discover any general characteristic, which belongs in common to absolutely all right action, no matter how different they may be in other respects (p. 35)?

He admits that this question is extremely difficult (p. 36), but he still feels that it is well worth distinguishing which are the more important theories. Even if the truth cannot be ascertained, Moore wants to decide which views are closer to the truth. Later writers gradually become more interested in simply discussing a view and less interested in offering personal appraisal and decision. The tide turned since the time Moore first urged what was then a difficult program, and the analysis of terms is the easier job. What needs to be urged is that we begin once again the difficult task of trying to appraise the author's own decision. Analysis can travel an easier route; it is more difficult to find a philosopher who will commit himself or herself as to the truth of an ethical standard as a guide for conduct.

What is interesting to note is that in Moore's analysis of Utilitarianism he distinguishes six different cases of possible action, not meaning (p. 39). Although his method is close to later analysis, the stress is upon the characteristics of action, not upon the characteristics of terms. However, Moore ends with a curious point which is more akin to analysis. He concludes by saying: "Whether this theory has ever been held in exactly the form in which I have stated it, I should not like to say" (p. 59). What he has done is to stress the analysis of action, but all of this becomes a little academic if no one actually adopts the theory he has been examining. You cannot, then, be very serious about action itself while remaining indifferent to its real acceptance. The stress is supposedly upon action, but if there is no concern for the reality of action, the interest is in theory for the sake of theory, analysis of terms for the sake of clarity.

Santayana has been acknowledged to be quite perceptive of shifts in philosophical interests, and in 1913 he has already noticed the shift away from any direct attention to the facts of moral life. Speaking of Russell, he discerns that "The author's estrangement from reality appears in his treatment of egoism..." (p. 268). Santayana objects to the logician's habit, as he says, of turning men into letters, and this is only important as one aspect of a strange phenomenon. That is, empiricists talking about a world which is, in reality, very far from actual moral experience.

Even more important, Santayana notes a touch of intolerance in the ethics of Moore and Russell, and he adds: "One trembles to think what it may become in the mouths of their disciples" (p. 269). Actually, having lost real conviction in the truth of any one standard, the discussion seemed characterized more by an indifference about modes of conduct than by intolerance. Santayana's prediction became true in a more subtle way, however: in a lack of tolerance for those who do not pursue philosophy along the lines of methodology. Moore stressed method, and it is quite appropriate that it is more over method than over doctrine that his successors were likely to be intolerant.

Shifting to 1930, we find Ross proposing to examine the conceptions that are central to ethics. Ross sounds quite similar to Moore. But as he proceeds he too is less interested in attempting to arrive at a single true definition than in simply distinguishing several possible meanings. In one step further removed, Ross passes from an interest in definition to an interest in the intention of the user of the definition, and a touch of arbitrariness begins to enter (p. 167). Terms, not conduct, are unmistakably paramount. The shift from ethical action per se to the intent of the user of ethical terms becomes even clearer in 1933 when Barnes states the emotive theory (p. 391). The terminology of exclamation and persuasion might not sound familiar to Moore, but the connection is direct.

To one who did not follow this development, it might seem odd that Moore's innocent suggestion for the use of analysis and definition as an instrument could eventually take over the whole province of ethics. But in 1935 Field examines the place of definition in ethics and concludes: "So the place of definition in ethics appears to be co-extensive with the greater part of its field" (p. 98). It is true that Field goes on to talk about moral experience, but definition is his real interest and the rest is merely homage to conventional issues. Moore had indeed stressed the question of how "good" is to be defined, but this is not the same as saying that problems of definition are almost identical with philosophical ethics. It is interesting to speculate on what part Wittgenstein might have played in developing this trend had he entered in.

In 1936 Campbell evidences the increasing indifference of philosophers in reaching a definite ethical conclusion. Not only does a positive theory not appear, he admits that his paper has deliberately "...set out to be no more than destructive" (p. 644). Such an attitude is almost shocking in ethics, where one is hardly able to be indifferent and where construction of a moral standard ought to be the aim. To be destructive as a preliminary examination is perhaps acceptable. But is there a new and vital ethical standard constructed by the discussion as a result of such destruction?

When Ayer begins to write about ethics (specifically 1936), the line of evolution from Moore becomes almost complete. Whether or not Ayer is representative of the newer generation is not important. The point is that he voices what seems to be a view quite different from Moore's but which actually is the development of a strain that Moore himself began. Ayer drops the use which Moore gave to linguistic analysis and asserts that "A strictly philosophical treatise on ethics should therefore make no ethical pronouncements" (p. 394). The subtleties of the various shifts in Ayer's later position are not important here. The point is that Ayer's view is closely connected with Moore's work earlier in the century, even though the latter wanted the philosopher to enter the moral life while the former takes away the ethical aim of ethics by dividing it between logic and social psychology.

Except to someone so steeped in this development in ethical theory that he or she takes its general direction for granted, surely it is evident that something has gone wrong with ethics when it is completely reduced to non-ethical terms. There is something contradictory about such an attempt, and yet Ayer says that "What we are interested in is the possibility of reducing the whole sphere of ethical terms to non-ethical terms" (p. 394). Ethics so transformed becomes some other branch of philosophy, and it cannot be expected to have any influence on the individual moral life.

Ethical statements have always been highly controversial. Thus when Ayer tells us in 1936 that on his view it is impossible to dispute about questions of value (p. 399), should we not suspect that this can only be true of an ethics which has been changed into something else? In the real world ethical issues are highly debatable, so any ethical theory which concerns this world cannot be at all pertinent without being controversial. Ayer is quite open about admitting that ethics has now been changed into something else (p. 401), but it isn't this the time to ask whether such ethical theory can serve its most needed function? And this is something of which we knew Wittgenstein felt in need.

With the emphasis on analysis, there is an increasing tendency to question the question without ever joining the argument. Stevenson says (in 1937) that the first thing to do is to examine the questions themselves, and he admits that this takes you no further than the preliminaries (p. 415). Evidencing this increasing lack of energy to face the more disputable areas in ethics, Stevenson admits that he will deal almost entirely with non-moral uses of good, "... only because it is simpler" (p. 423). Compare this with Wittgenstein's search for simplicity. The examination of the non-moral aspects of value terms will undoubtedly yield more that is concrete and can be agreed upon, but it certainly throws little light upon the complexities of individual moral dilemma. In the *Tractatus* Wittgenstein had other reasons for excluding ethics from technical philosophy, but the result is the same—until he begins to move toward the *Investigations*.

With Stevenson and Ayer a sense of arbitrariness has been introduced into ethical theory which seems out of keeping with the seriousness of the subject. Such phrases as "...it will be more convenient to use the expression..." appear more often. Reading such remarks one feels that the philosopher does not take his responsibility to society very seriously. Cleverness in the use of expressions has become standard, and such procedure leaves the impression that many contemporaries are writing strictly to excite the interest of other professional philosophers. They have lost sight of philosophy's larger tasks within society and within the general history of thought. The same can be said of Wittgenstein, at least in part, although he brooded over this missing aspect.

With the tendency to take ethical theory further away from the facts of moral life and to divide it up among logic, linguistics, and social psychology, there goes a parallel tendency for the ethical writer not to involve himself in his or her own discussion. Ewing says (in 1939) that, "This article is not intended to state what I positively believe to be true, but to make a suggestion which I think well worth while working out" (p. 231). His indecision about his own position is indicative of the increasingly non-moral nature of ethical writing. However, "real moral life" is such that a participant cannot really enter and remain neutral.

Ewing hints at an important point here when he remarks, "It is a curious fact that the controversy between naturalists and their opponents has centered rather around "good" than around "ought" (p. 234). Earlier in the century "ought" figured as prominently as "good," and it is no accident then, that the controversy centered increasingly around "good." For "good" is a term which may be either moral or non-moral, so that it was possible to treat it in non-moral value terms. On the other hand, "ought" is irrevocably connected to the dilemmas of the moral life. However important it may be to understand "good," no ethical theory is complete without a full-dress treatment of "ought." Obligation is the stuff of which the moral life is made, as the constant stringency which Wittgenstein enforced upon himself indicates. Ethical theory is certainly simpler if "ought" is relegated to social psychology or some other realm. But we are left with a serious question of whether the ethical theory that remains can fulfill its social obligations.

In 1944 Broad candidly announces that his topic was the epistemology of moral judgments (p. 363). No one would deny that, as Broad says, "Questions of epistemology and of logical analysis are interconnected" (p. 363). The issue is how far ethics may be turned into questions about sense data ("color" for Wittgenstein) without losing itself. After treating values like sense qualities, Broad says, "so much for the dialectics of the matter" (p. 386). At this point only a page of the article is left, and the result of the paper is that ethical questions become primarily epistemological ones. The topic of ethics had been inherited, but increasingly it was turned into the specialty of the day, whether it be logical analysis or empirical epistemology. There is no doubt that we now have logical dialecticians, but the question is whether there are ethicists as such. An ethicist is one who would work quite closely with the immediate facts of moral life, whereas logic and epistemology are by their nature more abstract and further removed. Wittgenstein eventually swung toward a pragmatic view, but his personal concentration on the moral life cannot be doubted.

When one reads Ewing (1947) on *Different Meanings of "Good" and "Ought"* (p. 210), we seem to have reached a stage in the argument in which the discussion has largely degenerated into the participants involved in the internal criticism of each other's views. The whole discussion at this point would have only minimum value for anyone unfamiliar with the details of its various evolutions. What is left is a lengthy intramural discussion that is supported by, and has meaning for, only the philosopher of a particular background and disposition. Philosophical discussion by its nature certainly moves away from immediate experience, but there may be something wrong with its initial direction when it continues to move away from all experience, rather than returning to make contact with the moral life and to clarify it, the resolution which Wittgenstein sought all his life. It is hard to see how anyone who read Ewing in isolation at this point could be seriously aided in any crucial moral decision.

H. D. Lewis notes this tendency of ethical theory to lose any direct relationship to moral experience. He observes that "...the problem of freedom is barely mentioned in two of the most influential books in recent years" (p. 576). The cause of this development comes to light when he remarks that "...Moore is much more concerned with the idea of value than with that of rightness or obligation" (p. 576). Moore never lost his conviction of the centrality of rightness for ethical theory. But since he centered his analysis upon non-ethical value, it was easy enough for later writers to turn ethics into a non-moral study.

Thus, when Feigl writes on ethics in 1950, he can turn the discussion almost wholly into a psychological vein (p. 667), and this will not seem inconsistent with the general current of discussion. Psychologists carefully refrain from issuing ethical pronouncements. But since philosophers are supposed to deal with ethical controversy, they cannot fulfill societies expectations if they in turn adopt psychological analysis. When Sellars in 1951 discusses obligation, the stress is so heavily on the analytic schematicism (p. 511) that it seems almost unimportant that a morally significant word is used. And when the discussion does touch on controversial issues, Sellars dismisses it as taking him too close to metaphysics (p. 517). It is hard to see how such a timid ethical theory can benefit the society which supports its activity, and certainly philosophy, as Wittgenstein found it in his time, seemed unable to give him support.

(3) The ethical and the logical-analytic questions split and then confused (1930-1951).

What happened first was that the logical analysis which Moore emphasized was split off from the traditional moral ethics, and then logical analysis was elevated until it was mistaken for the substance of ethics. One lesson taught by this history of events is that a stress on methodology may fail in ethics, since ethics is one field in which the material (i.e., the dilemma of the moral situation) is more important than the method. Various material questions cannot be interchanged in an established methodological treatment without losing their distinctively ethical character. The concentration on methodology, then, is perhaps most successful in epistemology, while least successful in ethical theory or in philosophy of religion. In ethics the subject matter is more important than the method by which it is treated. Wittgenstein knows this, places emphasis on method, and in so doing places ethical concerns outside philosophy's domain.

One conclusion seems to be that ethical questions can be detected by their tendency to involve the author and his methodology in the heart of the controversy. When writers become detached and noncommittal, it is a sure sign that they must be moving further away from the goal of ethical inquiry. Ethics is characterized by the impossibility of detached neutrality. The philosopher does not allow himself or herself to follow passion as its slave, but he or she cannot deal with it without feeling its effects. Therefore, if any analysis of ethical theory does not carry with it some impact on action, whether direct or indirect, it is "ethical" in name only. Wittgenstein also wanted to test the word by the deed, when he found intellectual schemes in themselves personally unsatisfactory.

When ethical theory reaches this state, in which it has little relevance for action or decision, the "plain man" (or "ordinary language") so often spoken of in the theory has been replaced by an isolated intellectual playing an intramural game—which is an "academic" affair in the popular sense of that term. The moral philosopher ought not to be as perplexed as the ordinary individual. But something is wrong when the philosophical endeavor has little of significance to say to the man or woman (or to the practitioner) involved in an actual moral struggle. When one asks whether he or she is morally justified in taking one's own life, he or she brings up a moral dilemma which involves more than a distinction of terms. Philosophy is certainly not a counseling service, but it is a proper question to ask what moral guidance a person might derive from a study of the ethical theory. Even Wittgenstein came to feel philosophy's detachment from his life, and he rebelled against academic philosophy.

What many philosophers have perhaps forgotten is that we are not as free to change the nature of our enterprise as we would perhaps like to be. Definitions can be changed at will, but the experience from which philosophy rises has characteristics too definite for any arbitrary procedure. Philosophy began as, and will continue to be, an attempt to solve the complicated questions which life always poses. The moral philosopher, then, is free to change the character of his enterprise, but never so that her theory does not return to give an account of the difficulties of moral decision.

A sense of the arbitrariness of logical play seems out of place in ethical theory, since the task of the ethicist is to establish norms capable of dealing forcefully and effectively with moral action. Where ethical questions are concerned, the philosopher should never be rigid or insensitive to views other than his own. Nevertheless, no matter what dialectical skills we possess, we seek to know where we stand in regard to the rightness and wrongness of conduct, a burden from which Wittgenstein never found release.

What we have a right to require of ethical theory is this: that it provide effective guidance and direction for ethical action and a means for some relief from our moral dilemmas. If, then, a theory lacks concern for our human moral situation, it is no longer "ethical," however interesting it may be for other reasons. As Wittgenstein followed—and perhaps accentuated—this drift, he became increasingly disenchanted with philosophy's value.

Looking back, it becomes obvious that he could not find, in the philosophy of his time and place, the way to move beyond the confines of his *Tractatus* in order to deal with "the mystical." This had always been of interest, but it came to border on a crises as the moral pressures internal to his life accelerated. And it should be clear why he found on release in the ethical theory of his time.

B. Tractatus Metaphysico-Theologicus [3]

While it is true that, as Wittgenstein taught us, what can be said can be said clearly, the logic of our language is such that we cannot know that it permits us to say everything that resolves our ethical pressures. However, the symbolic quality of language enables us to refer to, and to direct attention toward, that which is beyond language, perhaps even beyond its grasp, as Wittgenstein stated emphatically. The result is that, while what is said within a language may be said perfectly clearly, languages may also refer beyond themselves to structures which either are not clear in themselves or not so clear to us. If we avoid this extension, it is possible for the logical structure of the language to remain clear; but its impact on the hearer may be clouded by the thought of that which lies beyond language. In this sense, what can be said may not always be said clearly—if we include the speaker/writer's self-reflection on what is said. Still, if we decide to use language to refer to something beyond itself which is not equally clear, we must always explain fully the reasons for our enforced partial silence. Religious language is born from grasping the reasons for such silence; metaphysical discourse comes from the determination to speak as clearly as possible.

We learn that the limits set upon thought are not as narrow as the limits set upon language, and the limits set upon the various expressions of thought fall somewhere in between. Language is in fact able to refer to what it cannot adequately express. One result is to observe that we can set a limit to language, because we can think both sides of such a limit. On the other hand, we cannot similarly set a limit for thought, since this is only done by coming up against what cannot be thought, as Wittgenstein said and as Kant had noted earlier. In this area in-between the logical limits of language and the ultimate failure of thought, all metaphysics and theological speculation (as well as most religious experience) lies. Each enterprise thinks beyond the basic language structure and reports back into it what thought learns through testing its own limits. Language ought to stop with as much clarity as it can achieve; thought is different. It continues until it is finally forced into silence.

---

[3] Adapted from an article which appeared in *The Modern Schoolman*, Vol. XLI, No. 4, May 1964, pp. 366-375.

THE OMISSION OF ETHICS, THE EXCLUSION OF THEOLOGY 145

The truth of any expression, then, may be determined as being possible, and it can often be assigned a degree of probability. But since thought varies in the extent to which it can go beyond language before being reduced to silence, the truth of any proposition within language may be determined. Yet the truth of any theory about language itself, and particularly about its limits, cannot be so firmly fixed.

As to the truth of the theory here communicated, it seems to me likely, possibly even definitive for a time. Any analyst who moves within language structure may reach what seems a final solution, but any metaphysician or theologian must rest content with providing only possible solutions. Their thought is such that they cannot express anything more definitive within language. The value of this brief concluding exposition, then, consists in the fact that through explicating one possible view it shows at the same time how many other possible solutions remain unexplored. It could only be otherwise if we could know whether or not there is at least one language that is able to express everything that is, as well as everything that is not. But such a conclusion, unfortunately, we can never reach by the internal study of any language, its grammar, or its particular forms of expression.

The world is everything that has become the case. It can be understood by comprehending and postulating what might have been the case, if the elements had been different or differently organized, together with how the present situation developed and what this allows as both possible and probable for the future. An organic whole has been, and is being, formed out of the totality of all possible states. At any given moment our world has become a totality of facts, but this could never be at the same time the totality of all possible states. Language works upon facts, whereas thought is oriented more toward possible states. What can in fact form our world is determined by what is possible, and this involves all the possible facts for our world, all that is possible for us, but by no means all that is per se possible. Metaphysical language expresses the forms of possibility. It thus naturally must move beyond the logical structure of propositions.

This totality of all that is possible determines, through its internal laws, what may become a fact and also what cannot become a fact in our given world. This totality of all that is possible exists in logical space and contains within itself all possible factual worlds. Within our own world, we may also divide it into fact and possible. Any possible within this framework can either become a fact or not become a fact, depending upon the operation of causal powers, both natural and human. And every other possible would remain just what it is, although our factual structure can be altered in one direction or another. The real world is this relationship between fact and possible, and to express the origin of this relationship is the continuing task of both metaphysical and theological discourse.

What is possible, what can become an actual fact within our world's structure, comes out of the existence of an absolutely infinite set of possibles continuously present in logical space. This absolutely infinite set of possibles is the combination of every entity or object which could conceivably come into factual existence without encountering an internal contradiction. It is essential to any entity or object that comes into factual existence that it be at the same time a constituent part of this absolutely infinite set of possibles. Every fact has, in this sense, a dual life, a dual existence, and a double set of relationships. Language is therefore forever involved in an irreducible duplicity of reference.

If our logic is constructed to reflect the structure of our actual world (rather than a possible, perhaps even preferable, world), it will be a logic in which some things are contingent, given the powers of human freedom. For even if an entity can be actualized out of our particular set of possibles, this potentiality is dependent upon some human or naturalizing agency, and this power may be contingent in its action. The actualization of any possible can, of course, appear as an accident, even when the context which it helps to shape is itself considered necessary. Metaphysics describes both the necessary and the possible actualizing powers, as well as the accidental or "chaotic."

Possibles which are actualized tend to take on the degree of contingency or necessity found in the framework within which they appear. Considered in itself, the degree of contingency or necessity of any given possible depends primarily upon the degree of steadiness of its actualizing power, plus the degree of freedom or chaos involved. To determine degrees of contingency-necessity, one must examine the individual possible in relation to its actualizing agency and then consider this against the factual context in which it appears. This being the case, our metaphysical language will tend to reflect differing degrees of contingency-necessity, depending upon how the individual event is approached. The basic structure of our world is necessary when considered in its context; but it is only contingent, with a certain degree of probability, when taken in relation to all the possibles and contingent actualizing powers.

Theological discourse lacks even contextual certainty, since it speaks about its subjects only in the context of all of the possibles considered absolutely. Theological language can exhibit certainty only when it speaks of the rules governing the possibles as a whole (God), but this does not help it to make factually certain statements. For this reason theological language can be metaphysically insightful but pragmatically weak. Religious discourse, in so far as it speaks of actual experience, achieves an individual form of certainty.

If an entity is one among the absolutely infinite set of possibles, its potential actualization depends upon its relation to the other possibles, the framework of our particular world, and the rules governing inclusion and exclusion, together with the degree of power and steadiness of its proposed actualizing force or forces. The expression of this situation is the business of metaphysical language. Logical discourse, on the other hand, treats entities merely as possibles. Logic may treat every possible, considering each as a fact in logical space, without regard for the possibility of impossibility of their actualization within our world or their degree of uncertainty. This makes the language of logic neat and uncluttered, although the metaphysician's exposition can never be. Theological language has the even more difficult task of combining logical simplicity (God's) with the more complex and uncertain language that is appropriate to the actual world, human religious experience and, secondarily, God's activity in relating to individuals or to groups.

It is not possible to think of any entity apart from its context within the absolutely infinite set of possibles, although we can consider it in isolation from our (or its) particular spatial and temporal context. This fact makes metaphysical and theological speculation possible and the linguistic structure of their expressions often unusual. If we can speak momentarily about an entity apart from its context in some particular set of possibles, still we cannot speak of it apart from the probability of its actualization, which is why theological language always has causal overtones. Since the basis for its probable actualization is also internal to any possible entity, it cannot be grasped or spoken of without indicating this fact. Religious discourse always expresses the degree and the power of the actualizing force it depicts as lying in an entity that is not always a part of our actual world. Thus, it speaks of operations and actualization different from, or even the interruption of, our actual order. Religious language necessarily tends toward the eschatological; it is a language of finalization and transformation.

Words may occur alone; but they are meaningful only in the context of some mode of discourse, be it logical, factual (scientific), or theological (speculative). This is because any property of an entity, which is what a word expresses, may appear independently; but in actuality it is dependent upon the necessary basic metaphysical structure in which it appears. Thus any language need not express metaphysics at any given moment, but it is nevertheless dependent on some metaphysical context to establish basic meaning. Any property is a necessary part of all possible sets of possibles, even when it appears and is spoken of independently. Thus, the momentary independence of all language is a form of dependence, insofar as all language is forced to represent some basic metaphysical structure in order to establish its meaning.

To know an entity fully would be to know in detail all the probabilities for its occurrence in every set of possibles. For such a task language is actually inadequate, since it is bound by the limits of contextual description. "To know" is in part to understand the occurrence of an entity within some set of possibles, in such a way that its possible occurrences elsewhere are both suggested and allowed for. For this task language is adequate, but it needs constantly to summon its full powers of expression in order to do justice to the possible flexibility and not to fall into the common linguistic fallacy of expressing an entity's nature in a manner more rigid that its actual existence. Language expresses definiteness and inflexibility easily (except poetic and symbolic expression); to express a possible range of occurrences of a possible entity with precision (vagueness being the weak statements of an entity's possible occurrences) is exceedingly difficult. It requires the exertion of a rare theological/poetic power over language.

That such a linguistic power may be exercised is due to the fact that, within the nature of every particular set of possibles, the possibility of every possible combination is also to be found. As Plato expressed it, the very nature of an entity involves and is determined by all the possible states which at that moment it is not (Cf. the *Parmenides*). This necessary involvement of the full extent of nonbeing in being gives language its force, its range, it power—but also its problems and its imprecision. Either metaphysically or linguistically, it is not possible to concentrate upon one entity to the exclusion of all others, nor upon an actual state to the exclusion of all possible states. Theologically, language is in fact committed to attempting to grasp an entity in its setting among the absolute infinity of possibles (the divine nature) and the powers which establish their laws (divine power and will). The difficulties inherent in ordinary discourse are a special and restricted case of the difficulties of theological language.

Analyzing language is an unending process, precisely because no actuality is finally ultimate. Starting from the accurate description of an actual state, a new possibility can always subsequently be found. This changes the context in which the actuality is grasped and begins the linguistic reformulating ever over again. The object remains its factual self; but, since language arises in the area between the possible and the actual, the process of continually discerning a new possibility keeps language in a state of constant reformulating. To know the internal qualities and possibilities of an object is relatively simple. But since "to know" also involves all of the possible external contexts for an object, the knowing of a given object can be relatively simple in the first sense while being theologically difficult in the second.

To know the full range of the possibles would also be to know every fact; but the mind has difficulty here, since ordinary language is not geared to such expression. On the other hand, to know every possible fact, although easier to express, would be to know some but by no means all possible entities. Both knowledge and language can be complete as to facts while remaining incomplete and inexpressible as to all possibles.

Every actual entity also exists in a set of possible entities. I can think and speak about any given entity as if such a set of possibles did not exist around it. But I cannot know or express its essence without grasping its place within some set of possibles. Since a spatial object must lie in some finite space, the spatial or visual description of an entity is always the easiest, the clearest, and the most amenable to our language structure, as the empiricists have always recognized. Yet since a point in space is actually to be defined as a place in which to consider actualizing possibles, any attempt to consider the space in which these lie (rather than the spatial object itself) will always lead to greater metaphysical difficulties and more complex (if not also less clear) linguistic expression.

Every possible state of affairs cannot be contained within an object; that is too much for any entity to bear. Only an absolutely infinite set of possibles could contain the possibility of every state of affairs, although it also contains possibles which cannot become a state of affairs because of internal inconsistencies (contradictions) that would produce power failure (continued non-being). Given an already actualized set of possibles (such as our world), the form of an entity is the conditions for its actualization and for its continuance within that actualized set. An "entity," then, is some possible which has become organically capable of achieving and sustaining actual existence. The duration and evolution of this state is a description of the entity's powers in relation to the powers operative in its actualized context. Theological discourse often expresses this as God's activity; metaphysically it may be expressed more impersonally.

Every linguistic formula applied to complex entities or situations can be analyzed into statements about their constituent parts and powers. Since possibles completely constitute these complexes, any linguistic description of a complex entity necessarily involves language in an attempt to understand all the possibles and their range. Possible entities, it is clear, form the substance of any world, which is an organic set of actualized possibilities capable of self-maintenance. "Possibles," then, are essentially organic entities capable of actual existence, together with the negative element of those which are not organically so capable (often referred to as destructive forces or "evil").

If the possibles in our world had not come into organic union, whether a proposition made sense would depend entirely upon whether it could be located within an absolutely infinite set of possibles. In this case, language could be used by, and would be meaningful to, only God. As for ourselves, we could only form a picture of our world as one possible set, but it would be impossible for us to declare any factual proposition made about it as being either true or false. Without the actual world as its given base, human language could describe possible states freely but could decide no factual cases surely.

It is clear that, however different from our actual world another possible world might be, it must have something—a logical form—in common with our actual world, so in that sense no possible world is completely unknown. This common form is the general structure (Wittgenstein called it "grammar") of the absolutely infinite set of possibles itself. That is, whatever variation of content is possible, no world could escape reflecting its origin by not embodying the general structure governing all possibles. In that way we are equally open to learn the general structure of our world by turning away from it to study the structure of all possibles or by discerning the actual framework upon which the possibles in our world appear. Language is a mixed thing, since it reflects both approaches.

"Substance" means any possible capable of sustaining an actualized existence within some framework. It is a logical possibility, that requires some actualizing power, plus a greater or lesser degree of self-maintenance. Only if some set of possibles had in fact gained an actualized form could there be a fixed frame to the natural world. Yet, considered in themselves, the possibles, the existents, and the actualized world are in essence one. Although they appear in different frames, their origin is one. The existent is the contingent, the variable; the actualized fact is a possible which has become fixed. A configuration of actualized possibles forms the framework of the natural world. Language mixes the actualized fact with the possible in an attempt to express the existent.

In the absolutely infinite set of possibles the arrangement is somewhat different. Entities stand apart from one another, like members of a family, some loosely, some as within a genus. In a genus, possible entities are combined in a definite way, and the way in which possible entities stand together within a group constitutes the structure of that possible class, sometimes called a family. The form is the possibility which that structure has for attaining actualized existence. Any fact has a structure that consists of the form of the groups represented in it, since that determines how the fact came into existence. Language can exhibit such a form.

The totality of the possibles that attain actual existence, together with the possibles related to them, is the natural world at that moment. Metaphysical language describes this; theological language gives an account of its origin out of other possible sets; religious language meditates on its future and its outcome and considers how the introduction of new possibles, either by divine or by human freedom, might alter the structure radically.

The totality of possibles which are actual at any moment sets the limits for the actualization of future possibles, the limits of empirical language, and range of future discourse. Actualized possibles, together with non-actualized possibles, are reality. And since its totality is absolutely infinite, language is oriented more toward limited fact than toward unlimited possibility. The possible that has come into actual existence we call a fact; a negative fact is the non-actual existence of a possible. Language combines the negative and the positive, often to our consternation.

When considered in themselves, possible entities may appear to be independent of one another. But they are not independent of the set by participation in which they are given definite form. However, their independence is such that, from the actual existence or nonexistence of any possible entity, we cannot infer the necessary existence or nonexistence of another but only its relative probability or improbability. Since possibles do not appear sufficient, when we speak of "total reality" we mean the absolutely infinite set of possibles plus its actualizing powers or agencies. In that sense to speak about any reality is to involve language in an infinity and to refer, at least indirectly, to God.

Our mind operates by making for itself pictures of sets of possible entities; we speak by selecting out certain possibles and their relationships and sketching them in words. Language is the picture of a possible set reflected in linear discourse. Any mental picture or verbal theory presents possible entities in some logical order, determining the existence of compossibles and the non-existence of non-compossibles. Any such picture or theory is one possible mode of reality, and the function of language may be said to be to present possible models as more or less actual. What structure the picture corresponds to is determined by the set or sets of possibles it contains. The sets of possibles in the picture stand in the theory for structures which have or could become real. In this sense metaphysical language is always symbolic or pictorial; religious language is similarly pictorial, but it is oriented more toward possible structures than toward those already actualized. Many religious followers mistake this fact and are disappointed when what they believe fails to become literally true.

A theory or picture is distinguished from other statements by the fact that in it sets of possibles are combined with one another in a definite way, so that further statements can be deduced and predictions made from it. Such a picture or theory is itself one item among the possibles, so that often it is difficult to tell whether the theory applies merely to possibles or to actualities as well. Language also is subject to this same uncertainty; and its chief source of confusion comes from an inability to determine that toward which a particular discourse is primarily oriented—to the merely possible, to the partially actual, or to the fully actual.

Linguistic clarity of orientation is difficult to achieve, since a theory or picture means a definite combination of sets of possibles in a way that entities could be related to one another in actual existence. Since the function of a theory is to exhibit a relationship in which sets of possibles could become actual, in verbalizing the theory (describing the picture serially) it is easy to slip over into a different mode. The speaker implies that actualities are in fact organized in this way, when they may or may not be, or may be so to a greater or to a lesser degree.

Since the mind's natural orientation is toward possibles, when it thinks a theory or forms a picture it may easily hold it in suspension without prejudice as a merely possible form of organization. But when we speak, when we commit a picture to words, the theory has in that sense achieved for itself a state of actuality. As it is verbally pushed out into the world, it has a greater tendency to take upon itself the air of a description of actualities rather than a probable organization of possibles. Thus speech does make braggarts of us all.

Language commits us to theories in a way in which mere thought never does. In that sense language is more akin to physical prowess, whereas thought retains the uncertainty that governs possibility as a whole. Language commits us, just as our bodies commit us to this world; thought withdraws us from commitment because, in its own world, it constantly moves among new alternatives. Metaphysical language expresses this situation of thought; religious language seeks to stand between body and thought, between commitment and possibility, between action and personal resolution.

There is a possibility that any theoretical structure could in fact be the plan of our actual existence; we call this the usefulness or applicability of such a picture. Thus, applicability is the possibility that actualized, or potential entities, can be combined with one another after the manner of the sets of possibles of that picture. In this way any theory is linked with another after the manner of the sets of possibles of that picture. Theory is also linked with actualized reality in this way, too.

Or more properly, in this way we attempt to forge the link between theory and reality. Theory reaches up to actuality from the possible. Organizing theories is like developing a scale, one graduated from the possible to the actualized existence. As a bare minimum, in order to be a theory a set of possibles must have something in common with the actualized facts which it pictures, that to which it claims to apply. Between the picture and that which is pictured there must be some possible entities (now become factual or potential) which are identical, in order for the one to be a theory about the other at all. Fortunately, language is able to express the overlap of one realm upon the other, as well as to speak purely internally about a viewpoint. Unfortunately, language can be misleading if this tentativeness is not explicit.

What must a theory have in common with actualized reality in order to be able to represent it more or less closely? Clearly the theory must have the form of the same connection between sets of possibles which actualized reality has, not some other possible form of connection. In this case, the theory or picture or symbol can represent every actualized state whose form of connection it has. What we want to know from the theory is what is possible in the world and that, within these forms, certain relations and actions are possible, while within other forms they may not be.

Thus, a theory is rendered useless, however intriguing it may be, unless it does contain the form of connection between sets of possibles that is actually present in our world. A theory or symbol or picture, however, cannot represent directly its own form of connection with other possible theories; it shows it forth by being what it is and by the ability of language to ring changes on the theory, variations that carry it toward related theories. The power of language, although it can appear fixed, lies in its ability to exhibit the relations of possibility from which any theory comes.

A verbal picture must represent possibles from without. Its standpoint is one form of connection between possibles. Therefore the theory, being not totally internal to the world of possibles, can reflect within itself how nearly like or unlike it is to our own set of actualized possibles. But the picture cannot place itself outside all possible forms of connection that can exist between all the sets of possibles. And so, unfortunately, no final theoretical formula is possible. Language, therefore, shows no tendency to stop, least of all to stop itself. An infinite number of theoretical viewpoints is possible; thus metaphysical language tends to incompleteness and indecision.

Only a few of the possible theoretical structures could in fact be related at all closely to our actual world; thus religious language may be concrete and definite if it speaks about or leads to human embodiment. Through the definite activity of God's choice, which is what religious language expresses, metaphysical language is allowed some precision, some momentary singularity of perspective on the infinity of possibles that stand always before the mind. Oddly, then, religious language can achieve a form of definiteness and power that ordinary language seldom attains.

Another "Concluding Unscientific Postscript"

Kierkegaard gave this title to one book of his as a parody on the notion that anything philosophical/theological could ever be completed. We know that Wittgenstein said just before his death, "Tell them I've had a good life." In the sense of being productive, stimulating, even revolutionary in thought, we know that to be a true statement. But in the sense of reconciling his personal goals with the paradoxes and conflicts in his life, we know that this was ended only by the arbitrariness of death, as the Existentialists like to say, and not by a resolution or conclusion in any systematic sense.

Kierkegaard also asked himself: "But what is my opinion on these matters?" (in *The Philosophical Fragments*). He answered that to have an opinion was both too much and too little for him, since it suggested a life of peace, a final conclusion, and such was not his lot in the life of the spirit. Nor was it Wittgenstein's. A "concluding remark" should not settle the whole matter but rather should only start up the music again for the dance of life. Wittgenstein's ultimate gift to us, then, is neither the conclusiveness of the *Tractatus* nor the novel suggestions of the *Investigations* and his later fragmentary writings, but rather the constant struggle to contain and to express "the mystical" within thought.

"Mysticism," or "the mystical," means many things, of course. Plato pointed out that all significant concepts have multiple and not single meanings. The irony is that for both Wittgenstein and all of history's "mystics" that experience lies outside normal confines and thus is outside of normal language, it cannot be finally pinned down in its meaning within language. Wittgenstein recognized this fact early on, but he did not rule "the mystical" to be outside of human import, as some might try to do in order to simplify philosophy and to allow for its completion. One of our problems is that our "prophets" and our "seers" are connected to "the mystical," although not necessarily to any individual mystic. Why? Because both see and experience something beyond the confines of the ordinary world.

For just this reason Wittgenstein's "journey," or our journey with him, can neither be marked out in advance nor outlined so as to achieve a universal conclusion, much as Modern Philosophy has sought that. Following him there can be no fixed boundaries or paths just because "the mystical" never was excluded from his life. It can even be said to have become Wittgenstein's driving source, the origin of his "passion," as Kierkegaard might say. Thus, this writer had no idea what conclusion might be possible in advance of this writing, since all philosophizing with Wittgenstein should be a "life adventure," just as it was for him.

Along the way, any creative unorthodox thinker, such as Wittgenstein, will certainly suggest novelties to his attentive reader. This means, as he noted, one who puts the same personal energy into exploring the author's work that the author first did in writing it. The novel ideas in this essay first came for this author/follower by reading Tolstoy again to see what Wittgenstein found there of such significance and next by reviewing Kierkegaard and Augustine to see the often overlooked parallel in the life and work of these men whom Wittgenstein admired but whom most of his followers ignore. William James' "Pragmatism" also illuminates Wittgenstein's neglected stress on truth by enactment where ethics and religion are concerned.

However, what emerged most clearly to this "fellow traveler" was "the Gospel of Wittgenstein." As readers of the New Testament know, "gospel" means "the good news." It offers new ways of living and thinking to those who hear "the word" and accept it. Wittgenstein himself has been heard and accepted, but the major difference is that his is an "incomplete gospel." This is because what he sought and yet saw to be outside the confines of a technical philosophical/logical structure—this he could never find a way to incorporate into his own life in order to find the sought for resolution.

Followers of any famous or fruitful thinker may be slavishly meticulous, sorting out the details that the original inventive mind did not have time to do and may not have seen. Or, they may extend and move beyond, perhaps by taking a cue from what one recognizes as sought for but unachieved in the earlier thought-product. Aristotle bears many similarities to his teacher, Plato, but it is clear that he took over unfinished or difficult areas in the *Dialogues* and moved them in quite different directions. Thus, in speaking of "We Platonists" Aristotle included himself, but he knew his teacher to be suggestive not dogmatic.

Wittgenstein overlapped "prime time" in the Era of Empiricism and Modern, empirical-scientific oriented thought. But he marched to a different internal drummer from either the Vienna Circle or British Empiricism. Thus, ironically, he probably is one of the first "postmoderns" without meaning to be or intending it. He has been hailed as putting to rest both speculative philosophy and the unending question of "what is philosophy." And yet, as I hope has been shown, much of his life and work in fact opened up philosophy to all of "life's problems" and, thus, all that lies beyond the possibility of final confinement within any language.

The ultimate irony might be this: most followers treat Wittgenstein's technical philosophy in total detachment from his "life situation," and yet it may be that his most important insights and contributions can only be understood within his life-as-lived.

BIBLIOGRAPHY

anonymous,	*Cloud of Unknowing*, Trans. Clifton Walters. Penguin Books, Middlesex, England, 1961
Anscombe, G.E.M.,	*An Introduction to Wittgenstein Tractatus*, Harper & Row, 2nd ed., New York, 1965
Anselm,	*Appendix in Behalf of the Foll*, trans. by Deane, Open Court, Chicago, 1939
Augustine,	*Concerning the Teacher*, trans. by Leckie, Appleton-Century, New York, 1938
Ayer, A.J.,	*Wittgenstein*, University of Chicago Press, Chicago, 1985
Black, Max,	*A Companion to Wittgenstein's Tractatus*, Cornell University Press, Ithaca, New York, 1964
Bonaventura,	*The Mind's Road to God*, trans. by Boas, Liberal Arts Press, New York, 1953
Dionisius the Areopagite,	*The Mystical Theology*, trans. C.E. Rolt. SPCK Press, London, 1934
Epstein, Perle,	*Kabbalah*. Shambhala, Boston, 1978
Fann, K.T.,	*Wittgenstein's Conception of Philosophy*, University of California Press, 1971
Fogelin, Robert,	*Wittgenstein*, Routledge & Kegan Paul, London, 1976
Fogelin, Robert,	*Wittgenstein*, Routledge & Kegan Paul, London, 1976
Kenny, Anthony,	*Wittgenstein*, Harvard University Press, Cambridge, 1973
Kripke, Saul,	*Wittgenstein on Private Rules and Language*, Harvard University Press, Cambridge, 1982
Malcolm, Norman,	*Ludwig Wittgenstein: A Memoir*, Oxford University Press, London, 1958, 1962

Monk, Ludwig,	*Ludwig Wittgenstein*, Free Press, New York, 1990
Monk, Ray,	*Ludwig Wittgenstein: The Duty of Genius*, Free Press, New York, 1990
Moore, G.E.,	"Wittgenstein's Lectures in 1930-33," *Mind*, vol. I, LXIV, January, 1955, No. 253
Nyiri, J.C., ed.,	*Austrian Philosophy: Studies and Texts*, Philosophia Verlag, Munich, 1981
Pitcher, George,	*Wittgenstein: The Philosophical Investigations*, University of Notre Dame Press, Notre Dame, 1968
Plato,	*Charmides*, trans. by Jowett, Vol. I, New York, 1937
Plato,	*Protagoras*, Loeb Library trans., London, 1952
Plato,	*Cratylus*, trans. by Jowett, Vol. I
Plato,	*Theatetus*, Loeb Library trans., London, 1912
Plato,	*Phaedrus*, Loeb Library trans., London, 1914
Plato,	*Republic*, trans. by Cornford, p. 228, Oxford, New York, 1947
Plato,	*Epistle VII*, trans. by Post, Oxford, 1925
Plato,	*Sophist*, trans. by Cornford, Kegan Paul, London, 1949
Plato,	*Statesman*, trans. J.B. Skemp, Routledge & Kegan Paul, London, 1952
Quinton, A.M.,	*Wittgenstein's The Philosophical Investigations*, ed. George Pitcher, University of Notre Dame Press, Notre Dame, 1968
Scholan, G.,	*Kabbalah*, New American Library, New York, 1978
Scholem, Gershom,	*Major Trends in Jewish Mysticism*, Schocken Books, New York, 1941
Sellars and Hospers,	*Readings in Ethical Theory*, New York: Appleton-Century-Crofts, 1952
Sontag, Frederick,	"Plato, Unwritten Dialogue, The Philosopher" in *Proceedings of the XIIth International Congress of Philosophy*, Vol. II, Firenza, Italy, 1960, pp. 159-167

Sontag, Frederick,	"The Decline of British Ethical Theory," *Philosophy and Phenomenological Research*, Vol. XVIII, No. 2, Dec. 1957, pp. 219-227
Sontag, Frederick,	"Tractatus Metaphysico-Theologicus," *The Modern Schoolman*, Vol. XLI, No. 4, May 1964, pp. 366-375
Tolstoy, L.,	*The Complete Works of Count Tolstoy*, Vol. XV, "Short Exposition of the Gospel," AMS Press, New York, 1968
von Wright, G.H.,	*Culture and Value*, trans. Peter Winch, University of Chicago Press, Chicago, 1980
Wittgenstein, Ludwig,	*Notebooks, 1914-1916*, eds. G.H. von Wright, G.E.M. Anscombe, trans. Anscombe, Harper and Row, New York, 1969
Wittgenstein, Ludwig,	*Philosophical Investigations*, trans. G.E.M. Anscombe, Macmillan, New York, 1953
Wittgenstein, Ludwig,	*The Blue & Brown Books*, Basil Blackwell, Oxford, 1958
Wittgenstein, Ludwig,	*On Certainty*, trans. Paul & Anscombe. Basil Blackwell, Oxford, 1969
Wittgenstein, Ludwig,	*Remarks on Frazer's Golden Bough*, trans. A.C. Miles and Rush Rhees, Brynmill Press, Nottinghamshire, 1979
Wittgenstein, Ludwig,	*Notes* edited by Cyril Barrett, University of California Press, Berkeley, 1967
Wittgenstein, Ludwig,	*Philosophical Remarks*, Ed. Rush Rhees, trans. R. Hargrave & R. White, University of Chicago Press, Chicago, 1975
Wittgenstein, Ludwig,	*Philosophical Remarks*, eds. Rush Rhees, trans. Anthony Kenney, University of California Press, Berkeley, 1974
Wittgenstein, Ludwig,	*Remarks on the Foundation of Mathamatics*, eds. G.H. von Wright, R. Rhees, G.E.M. Anscombe; trans. Anscombe, MIT Press, Cambridge, 1967
Wittgenstein, Ludwig,	*Wittgenstein's Lectures, Cambridge 1930-32*, ed. Desmond Lee, University of Chicago Press, Chicago, 1980

Wittgenstein, Ludwig, *Wittgenstein's Lectures, Cambridge, 1932-35*, ed. Alice Ambrose, The University of Chicago Press, Chicago, 1982

Wittgenstein, Ludwig, *Zettel*, Edited by G.E.M. Anscombe, G.H. von Wright; trans. G.E.M. Anscombe, University of California Press, Berkeley, 1970

Wittgenstein, Ludwig, *Remarks on Color*, ed. G.E.M. Anscombe, trans. McAlister & Schätte, University of California Press, Berkeley, 1978

Wittgenstein, Ludwig, *Last Writings*, 3 vols., ed. von Wright and Nyman, trans. Luckhardt & Aue, University of Chicago Press, Chicago, 1982

Wittgenstein, Ludwig, *Letters to Russell, Keynes and Moore*, ed. von Wright, Cornell University Press, Ithaca, 1974

Wittgenstein, Ludwig, *The Zohar*, Ed. Gershom G. Scholem, Schocken Books, New York, 1963

Index

Abraham 91
abstraction 121
action 1, 3, 13, 16, 17, 22, 23, 46, 83, 86, 113, 121, 127, 134, 135, 136, 137, 138, 142, 143, 146, 153
aesthetic 13, 35, 54, 124
analysis 5, 12, 18, 22, 23, 28, 29, 33, 34, 36, 37, 40, 42, 46, 51, 56, 71, 86, 87, 95, 96, 97, 98, 101, 104, 105, 107, 108, 111, 113, 118, 129, 134, 135, 136, 137, 138, 139, 140, 141, 142
Anscombe 59, 60, 61, 62
Anselm 18, 100
Areopagite 91, 95
argument 52, 53, 113, 122, 135, 139, 141
ascetic practice 1, 41, 58, 72, 80, 81, 83, 89, 90, 105, 124, 125, 128, 129
atomism 4
Augustine 4, 11, 15, 16, 27, 28, 30, 39, 57, 64, 67, 70, 80, 91, 97, 99, 100, 102, 109, 126
Ayer 50, 51, 52, 138, 139, 140
Barnes 138
being 2, 3, 4, 16, 22, 24, 25, 36, 38, 39, 43, 46, 63, 66, 68, 74, 75, 76, 81, 94, 96, 97, 101, 107, 108, 109, 113, 114, 116, 117, 118, 119, 121, 129, 130, 139, 145, 146, 148, 149, 150, 154, 155
Bernard of Clairveaux 2
Bible 16, 20, 79
Black 10, 46, 47, 48
Bonaventure 47
Braithwaite 80
Brothers Karamazov 77
Camus 35, 105

certainty 13, 16, 17, 23, 61, 65, 66, 76, 78, 87, 124, 126, 127, 128, 129, 130, 147
Christian 3, 21, 25, 74, 76, 77, 87, 89, 91, 123, 131
Christianity 2, 20, 22, 23, 25, 26, 76, 89, 91, 94, 124, 127
Cloud of Unknowing 93, 94
color 15, 17, 27, 40, 41, 71, 82, 109, 129, 130, 141
commitment 1, 26, 51, 125, 153
complexity 11, 23, 27, 69, 106, 127
conception 14, 51, 52, 56, 66, 81, 92, 119, 127
Concerning the Teacher 4
conclusiveness 14, 21, 155
Confessions 11, 27, 39, 57, 64, 70, 80, 91, 126
consciousness 6, 22, 90
courage 3, 21
Cratylus 98, 100, 119
Culture and Value 19
dialectic 20, 45, 52, 117, 121
Dionysius 91, 92, 95
Dostoyevsky 57, 64, 105
dream 18, 23, 81
Epictetus 6, 7, 134
epistemology xi, 60, 106, 140, 141, 142
Epistle VII 101
Epstein 90
ethical xi, xii, 1, 3, 4, 7, 10, 12, 19, 27, 32, 40, 61, 70, 83, 90, 128, 133, 134, 135, 137, 138, 139, 140, 141, 142, 143, 144
ethics xi, 10, 19, 22, 37, 47, 49, 51, 54, 57, 59, 77, 79, 134, 135, 136, 137, 138, 139, 140, 141, 142
Euthydemus 119

Ewing 140, 141
existence xi, 18, 19, 21, 22, 35, 52, 76, 79, 89, 92, 94, 96, 97, 100, 116, 117, 121, 146, 148, 150, 151, 152, 153
existentialism 14, 69
existentialist 1, 22, 26, 67
Experience 2, 10, 13, 15, 27, 28, 29, 34, 36, 37, 38, 39, 43, 45, 48, 51, 55, 67, 70, 71, 73, 74, 75, 77, 86, 88, 93, 94, 109, 110, 120, 131, 134, 137, 138, 141, 143, 144, 147, 155, 156
Fann 52, 53, 57
Feigl 141
finality 5, 7, 9, 10, 12, 13, 16, 20, 27, 29, 34, 40, 41, 45, 49, 53, 70, 77, 79, 85, 86, 87, 92, 95, 103, 127, 128, 129, 130
Fogelin 4, 49, 50
forgiveness 2, 20, 22, 25, 27, 66, 67, 80
Frazer 17
freedom 129, 141, 146, 151
Frege xi, 9, 45, 59, 60, 61, 63, 70, 71, 72, 79
Freud 13, 17, 18, 86, 87, 107, 108
Geach 66
generality 14
God xi, 2, 3, 4, 6, 7, 16, 18, 20, 22, 24, 25, 26, 27, 33, 35, 39, 41, 42, 43, 46, 47, 48, 49, 52, 54, 61, 63, 65, 66, 67, 68, 74, 75, 77, 78, 80, 81, 83, 88, 89, 90, 91, 92, 93, 94, 95, 96, 106, 108, 110, 115, 124, 147, 150, 152, 154
Goethe 23, 83
Golden Bough 17
Gospel 74, 75, 123, 124, 126, 127, 131, 156
grammar 9, 12, 13, 27, 28, 29, 30, 31, 36, 37, 38, 39, 57, 64, 78, 79, 85, 98, 101, 104, 106, 110, 145, 150
guilt 3, 7, 20, 66, 82
happiness 26, 35, 76
Hegel 2, 5, 11, 14, 15, 20, 45, 53
Heidegger 28, 35, 107, 108
history 41, 63, 124, 127, 131, 133, 135, 140, 142, 155
holocaust 10, 48

Hume 18, 47, 109
individual 4, 14, 15, 27, 33, 43, 71, 74, 86, 110, 139, 143, 146, 147, 156
intellect 2, 4, 12, 21, 25, 26, 82, 92, 93, 94, 128, 129
intelligence 24, 56, 65, 71, 81, 92
irony 24, 68, 115, 155
James 2, 18, 20, 33, 43, 45, 51, 55, 70, 74, 75, 76, 156
Jesus 1, 12, 16, 20, 23, 24, 73, 74, 76, 81, 106, 109, 124, 128, 131
Jew 48, 88, 131
Jewish 21, 46, 87, 89, 91
Judaism 2, 89
justification 27
Kabbalah 87, 88, 91
Kabbalist 3, 28, 88, 89, 90, 91
Kant 36, 39, 45, 144
Kazanatzakis 2, 24
Kenny 52
Kierkegaard 1, 3, 4, 5, 6, 11, 12, 14, 15, 16, 19, 20, 21, 23, 25, 26, 27, 29, 30, 32, 33, 35, 38, 40, 41, 42, 45, 46, 50, 51, 52, 53, 55, 56, 57, 64, 66, 67, 70, 71, 73, 78, 82, 86, 87, 109, 155, 156
knowledge xi, 13, 16, 30, 60, 61, 64, 88, 89, 90, 92, 93, 96, 97, 98, 99, 100, 101, 108, 109, 117, 119, 120, 121, 128, 149
Kripke 52
language xi, 3, 6, 9, 10, 11, 12, 13, 14, 15, 16, 17, 18, 19, 20, 21, 22, 23, 27, 28, 29, 30, 31, 32, 33, 34, 35, 36, 37, 38, 39, 41, 42, 46, 47, 48, 49, 50, 52, 53, 54, 55, 56, 57, 59, 60, 61, 62, 63, 64, 70, 71, 72, 73, 76, 77, 78, 79, 80, 81, 83, 85, 86, 87, 88, 89, 90, 91, 94, 95, 96, 97, 98, 99, 100, 101, 102, 103, 104, 105, 106, 107, 108, 109, 110, 117, 125, 127, 129, 130, 134, 142, 144, 145, 146, 147, 148, 149, 150, 151, 152, 153, 154, 155, 157
Last Writings 41
Learned Ignorance 6, 48
learning 6, 13, 15, 56, 82, 89, 107, 114

Lessing 20
Lewis 141
life xi, xii, 1, 2, 3, 4, 5, 6, 7, 10, 11, 12, 13, 14, 16, 17, 18, 19, 21, 22, 23, 24, 25, 26, 27, 29, 30, 32, 33, 34, 35, 36, 38, 39, 40, 41, 42, 43, 46, 47, 48, 51, 52, 53, 54, 55, 61, 62, 63, 64, 65, 66, 67, 68, 69, 70, 71, 72, 73, 74, 75, 76, 77, 78, 79, 80, 81, 82, 83, 86, 87, 89, 90, 91, 93, 104, 105, 108, 109, 111, 119, 120, 121, 123, 124, 126, 127, 128, 129, 131, 134, 136, 137, 139, 140, 141, 143, 144, 146, 155, 156, 157
linguistic 5, 23, 28, 43, 56, 62, 76, 78, 85, 95, 110, 134, 138, 147, 148, 149, 150, 152
Locke 45
logic xi, 3, 7, 9, 10, 11, 14, 15, 16, 17, 19, 20, 25, 27, 28, 30, 31, 32, 33, 34, 36, 37, 38, 40, 43, 45, 46, 47, 48, 51, 53, 54, 55, 57, 59, 60, 61, 62, 63, 64, 67, 68, 71, 72, 73, 75, 77, 79, 85, 89, 103, 104, 105, 106, 109, 110, 117, 121, 127, 128, 139, 140, 141, 144, 146, 147
Longfellow 24
love xi, 21, 24, 26, 27, 35, 42, 65, 67, 68, 72, 74, 76, 81, 82, 89, 93, 94, 95, 104, 106, 120, 126, 127, 128, 129
Lysis 119
Malcolm 57, 62, 64, 65, 66, 67, 74
mathematics xi, 3, 6, 7, 13, 15, 16, 17, 19, 20, 23, 29, 30, 31, 32, 33, 34, 38, 45, 47, 48, 59, 60, 62, 63, 71, 80, 89, 104, 105, 107, 109, 110, 117, 127
Meno 4
Merton 65
Messianism 89
method 14, 16, 22, 27, 37, 38, 40, 43, 45, 52, 55, 56, 64, 71, 73, 74, 76, 80, 81, 82, 85, 86, 95, 96, 103, 104, 105, 107, 108, 109, 111, 113, 114, 115, 119, 120, 121, 122, 124, 125, 126, 127, 128, 129, 130, 134, 137, 142
Michelangelo 18
mind xi, 4, 12, 13, 19, 21, 24, 26, 27, 30, 32, 40, 41, 42, 47, 48, 52, 54, 57, 65, 66, 71, 72, 73, 74, 89, 91, 93, 98, 99, 100, 101, 102, 107, 108, 109, 118, 121, 128, 149, 152, 153, 154, 156
model 17, 19, 29, 33, 38, 54, 67, 104, 106, 107
Mohammed 131
momentary 20, 33, 148, 154
Monk xi, xii, 1, 2, 3, 5, 59, 66, 68, 69, 72, 73, 75, 81, 82, 83, 93, 120, 123
Moore 16, 56, 68, 134, 135, 136, 137, 138, 139, 141, 142
Moses 26, 131
music 21, 55, 70, 120, 155
Muslim 131
mysticism 3, 10, 51, 69, 75, 77, 85, 87, 88, 89, 90, 91, 92, 123, 126, 155
Nicholas Cusanus 6
Nietzsche 6, 15, 17, 20, 21, 103
Night 10
Notebooks 33
ontology 96
Parmenides 121, 148
Paton 59
Paul 23
perception 12, 27, 66, 71, 91, 118, 121
Phaedrus 101, 119, 120
Philosophical Fragments 11
Philosophical Grammar 30, 85
Philosophical Remarks 27, 30
Plato 4, 5, 21, 22, 31, 37, 53, 72, 94, 95, 97, 99, 101, 109, 111, 112, 113, 114, 115, 116, 117, 118, 119, 120, 121, 122, 129, 148, 155, 156
poetry 50, 64, 77, 78, 105, 107
Positivism 50, 51, 54, 56, 61, 62, 71
Pragmatism 13, 33, 46, 49, 54, 72, 156
progress 20, 47, 90, 93
proposition 15, 28, 29, 30, 31, 33, 34, 43, 49, 60, 61, 76, 85, 145, 150

Protagoras 100, 119
psychology 4, 15, 16, 17, 19, 40, 43, 55, 60, 71, 105, 139, 140
Quinton 5, 6, 48, 49
random 33
rational 2, 13, 18, 46, 67, 91, 93, 114, 122
reality 3, 9, 11, 30, 31, 32, 33, 34, 36, 37, 38, 39, 46, 47, 48, 54, 56, 60, 61, 71, 75, 76, 78, 79, 80, 85, 87, 89, 95, 96, 98, 101, 102, 103, 106, 109, 110, 114, 116, 117, 121, 137, 151, 152, 153, 154
religion xi, 3, 7, 12, 16, 17, 20, 25, 37, 39, 47, 48, 49, 50, 51, 54, 55, 57, 63, 64, 66, 67, 68, 70, 74, 76, 77, 79, 82, 125, 127, 142
religious 1, 2, 4, 7, 17, 18, 19, 20, 22, 24, 25, 26, 27, 32, 40, 45, 51, 66, 67, 70, 72, 73, 74, 75, 77, 80, 82, 83, 123, 125, 126, 128, 131, 144, 147, 151, 152, 153, 154
religious Belief 17
Renan 124
Republic 22, 99, 101, 120, 121
Rilke 42, 103
Ross 138
Russell xi, 9, 14, 45, 51, 53, 59, 60, 61, 63, 67, 68, 70, 71, 72, 73, 77, 79, 136, 137
salvation 2, 22, 25, 73, 75
Santayana 137
Schlick 50
Scholem 87, 89, 130
Schopenhauer 45, 59, 63, 70, 105
Sellars 142
Sex and Character xi
Sextus Empiricus 47
simplicity 6, 11, 23, 28, 65, 70, 124, 127, 128, 139, 147
Skjolden 75
Socratic 5, 21, 48, 55, 80, 98, 109
Sophist 98, 101, 112, 113, 115, 116, 117, 118, 119, 121, 122
Spinoza 16, 43, 45
spirit 12, 17, 20, 72, 111, 119, 121, 122, 155
Stevenson 139, 140

Stranger 112, 115
suicide 22, 25, 35, 75, 94, 105, 124
System 2, 5, 6, 13, 26, 29, 37, 46, 49, 55, 57, 62, 70, 71, 95, 104, 106, 109, 110, 127
systematization 11, 20, 45, 50
teaching 7, 12, 13, 18, 39, 47, 55, 65, 71, 72, 79, 89, 91, 97, 101, 103, 123, 124, 125
The Blue & the Brown Books 14
The Steps of Humility 2
the Tractatus 4, 5, 6, 7, 9, 10, 11, 12, 14, 15, 16, 20, 21, 34, 37, 39, 40, 41, 45, 46, 47, 48, 49, 50, 51, 55, 56, 57, 59, 60, 61, 62, 64, 65, 69, 70, 71, 72, 73, 76, 77, 78, 79, 80, 81, 85, 86, 87, 88, 89, 90, 92, 93, 94, 103, 105, 107, 109, 110, 111, 124, 127, 128, 129, 130, 139, 155
Theatetus 101, 121
theology 91, 95
theory xi, 3, 9, 18, 24, 33, 39, 45, 49, 50, 51, 53, 56, 60, 61, 72, 75, 78, 79, 82, 94, 103, 104, 105, 123, 133, 134, 137, 138, 139, 140, 141, 142, 143, 145, 152, 153, 154
thought xi, 2, 3, 4, 5, 11, 12, 15, 16, 17, 18, 20, 22, 28, 29, 31, 32, 33, 35, 37, 38, 40, 41, 42, 46, 51, 52, 56, 57, 59, 60, 61, 62, 63, 66, 67, 72, 73, 74, 76, 77, 80, 81, 83, 86, 90, 91, 92, 93, 94, 97, 101, 103, 105, 106, 107, 109, 111, 116, 119, 121, 122, 123, 128, 140, 144, 145, 153, 155, 156, 157
thought, 32
Tolstoy 21, 33, 45, 63, 64, 66, 67, 70, 75, 77, 123, 124, 125, 126, 127, 128, 129, 131, 156
Trappist 47, 67
truth 3, 17, 26, 33, 43, 60, 61, 62, 68, 71, 77, 78, 80, 92, 95, 101, 103, 104, 105, 106, 107, 108, 109, 110, 119, 120, 121, 123, 124, 125, 127, 128, 136, 137, 145, 156
unity 4, 14, 91, 114, 124

Vienna Circle 9, 10, 14, 19, 27,
    50, 51, 70, 71, 105, 127, 157
von Wright 19, 50, 62, 63, 64, 68
Weininger xi
Wiegel 10
Wittgenstein xi, xii, 1, 2, 3, 4, 5,
    6, 7, 9, 10, 11, 12, 13, 14, 15,
    16, 17, 18, 19, 20, 21, 22, 23,
    24, 25, 26, 27, 28, 29, 30, 31,
    32, 33, 34, 35, 36, 37, 38, 39,
    40, 41, 42, 43, 45, 46, 47, 48,
    49, 50, 51, 52, 53, 54, 55, 56,
    57, 58, 59, 60, 61, 62, 63, 64,
    65, 66, 67, 68, 69, 70, 71, 72,
    73, 74, 75, 76, 77, 78, 79, 80,
    81, 82, 83, 85, 86, 87, 88, 89,
    90, 91, 92, 93, 94, 95, 96, 100,
    102, 103, 104, 105, 106, 107,
    108, 109, 110, 111, 113, 115,
    116, 117, 118, 119, 120, 121,
    122, 123, 124, 125, 126, 127,
    128, 129, 130, 131, 134, 135,
    138, 139, 140, 141, 142, 143,
    144, 150, 155, 156, 157
Wittgenstein's Tractatus 59
Wittgenstein. xi
Works of Love 67
Zen 3, 10, 55, 58, 73
Zettel 33, 37, 39
Zohar 90, 91, 130

www.ingramcontent.com/pod-product-compliance
Ingram Content Group UK Ltd.
Pitfield, Milton Keynes, MK11 3LW, UK
UKHW041428180426
11947UKWH00007B/353